The Gypsies

The Gypsies

Titles in the Indigenous Peoples of the World series Include:

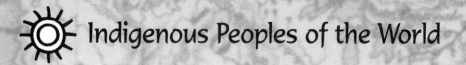

Indigenous Peoples of the World

The Gypsies

Anne Wallace Sharp

LUCENT
BOOKS®

THOMSON

™

GALE

San Diego • Detroit • New York • San Francisco • Cleveland • New Haven, Conn. • Waterville, Maine • London • Munich

LIBRARY OF CONGRESS CATALOGING-IN-PUBLICATION DATA

Sharp, Anne Wallace.
     The gypsies / Anne Wallace Sharp.
          p. cm. — (Indigenous peoples of the world)
Summary: Discusses the historical origins, beliefs, arts, family life, cultural clashes with
white Europeans, and future hopes of the nomadic Rom, or Roma, people who were
once called Gypsies.
Includes bibliographical references and index.
     ISBN 1-59018-239-1 (alk. paper)
     1. Romanies—Juvenile literature. [1. Romanies.] I. Title II. Indigenous peoples
of the world (San Diego, Calif.)
     DX118 .S46 2003
     909'.0491497—dc21

                                                                                    2002011935

Contents

Foreword

Nearly every area of the world has indigenous populations, those people who are descended from the original settlers of a given region, often arriving many millennia ago. Many of these populations exist today despite overwhelming odds against their continuing survival.

Though indigenous populations have come under attack for a variety of reasons, in most cases land lies at the heart of the conflict. The hunger for land has threatened indigenous societies throughout history, whether the aggressor was a neighboring tribe or a foreign culture. The reason for this is simple: For indigenous populations, *way of life* has nearly always depended on the land and its bounty. Indeed, cultures from the Inuit of the frigid Arctic to the Yanomami of the torrid Amazon rain forest have been indelibly shaped by the climate and geography of the regions they inhabit.

As newcomers moved into already settled areas of the world, competition led to tension and violence. When newcomers possessed some important advantage—greater numbers or more powerful weapons—the results were predictable. History is rife with examples of outsiders triumphing over indigenous populations. Anglo-Saxons and Vikings, for instance, moved into eastern Europe and the British Isles at the expense of the indigenous Celts. Europeans traveled south through Africa and into Australia displacing the indigenous Bushmen and Aborigines while other Westerners ventured into the Pacific at the expense of the indigenous Melanesians, Micronesians, and Polynesians. And in North and South America, the colonization of the New World by European powers resulted in the decimation and displacement of numerous Native American groups.

Nevertheless, many indigenous populations retained their identity and managed to survive. Only in the last one hundred years, however, have anthropologists begun to study with any objectivity the hundreds of indigenous societies found throughout the world. And only within the last few decades have these societies been truly appreciated and acknowledged for their richness and complexity. The ability to adapt to and manage their environments is but one marker of the incredible resourcefulness of many indigenous populations. The Inuit, for example, created two distinct modes of travel for getting around the barren, icy region that is their home. The sleek, speedy kayak—with its whalebone frame and sealskin cover—allowed the Inuit to silently skim the waters of the nearby ocean and bays. And the sledge (or dogsled)—with its caribou hide platform and runners built from whalebone or frozen fish covered with sealskin—made travel over the snow- and ice-covered landscape possible.

The *Indigenous Peoples of the World* series strives to present a clear and realistic picture of the world's many and varied native cultures. The series captures the uniqueness as well as the similarities of indigenous societies by examining family and community life, traditional spirituality and religion, warfare, adaptation to the environment, and interaction with other native and nonnative peoples.

The series also offers perspective on the effects of Western civilization on indigenous populations as well as a multifaceted view of contemporary life. Many indigenous societies, for instance, struggle today with poverty, unemployment, racism, poor health, and a lack of educational opportunities. Others find themselves embroiled in political instability, civil unrest, and violence. Despite the problems facing these societies, many indigenous populations have regained a sense of pride in themselves and their heritage. Many also have experienced a resurgence of traditional art and culture as they seek to find a place for themselves in the modern world.

The *Indigenous Peoples of the World* series offers an in-depth study of different regions of the world and the people who have long inhabited those regions. All books in the series include fully documented primary and secondary source quotations that enliven the text. Sidebars highlight notable events, personalities, and traditions, while annotated bibliographies offer ideas for future research. Numerous maps and photographs provide the reader with a pictorial glimpse of each society.

From the Aborigines of Australia to the various indigenous peoples of the Caribbean, Europe, South America, Mexico, Asia, and Africa, the series covers a multitude of societies and their cultures. Each book stands alone and the series as a collection offers valuable comparisons of the past history and future problems of the indigenous peoples of the world.

Who Are the Gypsies?

The Gypsies are a nomadic people whose ancestors came from India. Living and traveling in caravans of colorfully painted wagons, the Gypsies have always had an air of romantic mystery about them. Their lively music and dance, their colorful costumes, and their unusual professions, such as fortune telling, metal working, and street entertainment, have fascinated people for generations.

While the term "gypsy" with a small "g" is often applied to anyone leading a traveling life, the word "Gypsy" with a capital "G" denotes a distinct ethnic group. According to folklore historian James Riordan, "When Europeans first met them, some of the wanderers proudly said they were descendants of the Egyptians. So the British called them Gypsies."[1] The name stuck, despite the fact that the group had a far different origin.

Toward the end of the twentieth century, the Gypsies formally adopted the name "Roma," feeling that this title had a less negative connotation. While the word "Roma," or Rom as they are sometimes called, seems to refer to the country of Romania, there is no connection between the two.

The Gypsies

The Roma can trace their roots back to northwestern India. For a multiplicity of reasons, in the early tenth century several groups of people began to leave India, ultimately reaching Europe around the beginning of the fifteenth century.

"Gypsies," according to historians, "were the first people of color to come into Europe in large numbers. Having no country of their own . . . they were in every sense outsiders."[2] They were dark in appearance, spoke a strange and unfamiliar language, and practiced very different social customs than the people of Europe. There even were suspicions that the Gypsies were spies and that they possessed sinister magical powers. These suspicions and others made it difficult for the Gypsies to establish themselves in settled communities.

The Roma have always lived apart from mainstream society, mostly by choice, but also because of the widespread hostility with which they have been greeted. Adding to the problem, however, were the Roma's own feelings of distrust. The enormous differences between their language and that of the non-Roma made communication nearly impossible. On top of that, the Gypsies' strict traditional laws prohibiting contact or intermarriage with the non-Roma led to little opportunity for outsiders to understand the Roma way of life.

The resulting suspicions on both sides and the separation of the two cultures undoubtedly helped cause many erroneous and negative images and stereotypes of the Roma through the years. For instance, at one time or another the Gypsies have been accused of being sorcerers, child kidnappers, murderers, cannibals, and much worse. They have been referred to as lazy, ignorant, and worthless. They have been called animals, pagans (worshippers of more than one god), and heathens. These labels serve as indicators of the hatred that existed and continues to exist against the Roma throughout the world.

A History of Persecution

"The history of the Roma," writes historian David M. Crowe, "is a bittersweet

An artist's depiction of Gypsies, now called Roma, sharing a lighthearted moment. Europeans have long regarded the Roma way of life with suspicion.

tale that centers around centuries of mistreatment."[3] If one word, in fact, could be used to summarize the life of the Roma, it would be "persecution." At various times, writes *National Geographic* journalist Peter Godwin, who traveled with the Gypsies in the late twentieth century, "They have been forbidden to wear their distinctive bright clothes, to speak their own language, to travel, to marry one another, or to ply their traditional crafts."[4]

From almost the day the Roma arrived in Europe, discriminatory laws were passed, barring them from certain countries and certain occupations. In the centuries that followed, the Gypsies, regardless of where they went, were persecuted and often killed. According to historians, "The European states decided that the only way to deal with the Roma was to remove them by expulsion, repression, assimilation, and, later, extermination."[5]

These efforts would culminate during World War II when German dictator Adolf Hitler ordered the extermination of several ethnic groups, including people of Jewish and Gypsy descent. This period of time in world history is known as the Holocaust. It resulted in over one and a half million Roma deaths.

The Gypsies Today

Today, the prejudice and persecution continues. "The Roma remain to date," writes the European Roma Rights Center, an organization created to protect the Roma's civil rights, "the most deprived ethnic group of Europe. Almost everywhere, their fundamental rights are threatened."[6] Discrimination continues in every aspect of their lives, particularly in education, health care, and employment.

Today, there are between twelve and fifteen million Roma worldwide, although their actual numbers are probably higher. An exact count is impossible since many countries do not include them in their censuses. They live on every continent except Antarctica, but the largest concentrations of Roma can be found in Eastern Europe and Russia.

As the Roma enter the twenty-first century, they face a difficult and challenging future. Recent advances in education are beginning to have a positive impact, but the problems of poverty, unemployment, and discrimination have been harder to eradicate. For the first time in the history, however, governments and organizations around the world are hearing the voices of the Roma.

The Roma have survived over five hundred years of oppression by being resilient and by being able to adapt to the changing times. Today, they share a common heritage and a firm commitment to family and community, and they are beginning to adopt many Western ways of life while continuing and even resurrecting many of their ancient traditions.

Chapter 1

The Romaniya

The beliefs, customs, and traditions of the Roma are often referred to as the *Romaniya*. The *Romaniya* guides every aspect of Roma life, from their relationships with each other to their relationships with the non-Roma, or *gadje*. These customs have never been written down but rather have been passed down orally from one generation to the next.

It has been virtually impossible for historians to determine whether the *Romaniya* was a by-product of discrimination and persecution or whether the laws developed independently. Whatever the origin of the rules, the survival of the Roma has often depended on their adherence to these traditions, as only the strength of their community and family ties and their obedience to the "law" have stood between them and their near annihilation.

Having no universal Roma culture as such, each Roma community differs in small ways from other groups of Gypsies. All, however, stress strict adherence to the *Romaniya*. There also are three characteristics that are common to every group. First is a staunch loyalty to family and community. Second is the belief in God. Third, for the most part, is that the Roma have shunned the non-Gypsy world, frequently showing contempt for the laws and traditions of other societies, while maintaining their own strict code of behavior.

A Nomadic Life

From their earliest beginnings, the Roma have been a nomadic people, moving from place to place with the seasons. According to historians Eric Solsten and David E. McClure: "Preferring to feel free and unhindered, Gypsies attached little importance to the accumulation of property and wealth, choosing instead a life of wandering and bartering."[7]

W.R. Rishi, a Roma writer, reports the comments of a Gypsy man who was asked why he and other Gypsies preferred the nomadic life. The man responded:

I have been asked many times would I like to live in a house. This is something I just can't explain to people and make people understand, as living in a house is not my idea of life at all. I have lived in caravans—horse-drawn and trailer—all my life. I am a man of the wilds, of the open air, of the fields and the woods, and I could not be this if I lived in a house.[8]

The unwillingness of village and town officials in medieval Europe to allow the Roma to live permanently in any one area also led to the Gypsies' pursuit of a nomadic life. Roma scholar and activist Ian Hancock elaborates: "Gypsies in Europe have traditionally been kept on the move because of laws which have given them no alternatives."[9]

A small Gypsy caravan travels a road in South Wales in 1935. The Roma have traditionally lived on the move and have avoided mingling with other cultures.

Many Roma myths have arisen to explain the Roma's history of nomadism. There are tales that tell "of Roms who are descendants of the [black]smiths who made nails for the Crucifixion; or of Roms who stole the fourth nail from the cross," writes James Riordan, "or of the Roms hanged alongside Christ. That is why Roms were doomed to roam the earth."[10] Their constant wandering, another legend alleges, was their punishment for being among those who refused to help Joseph and Mary prior to Christ's birth.

Gypsy Caravans

The Gypsies have always been on the move, traditionally traveling in horse-drawn caravans. Typically, the men traveled toward the front of the entourage while women and children followed, often riding in open carts. Richer families often had elaborately carved caravans with narrow glass windows.

Roma travel was largely determined by the seasons. Most Gypsies began their journeys in the spring, stayed on the move during the summer and fall, and found campgrounds where they could settle in for the winter. These temporary locations or settlements were usually on the outskirts of towns and villages. The Roma wanted to be far enough away to stay separate from the non-Roma, but close enough so that the women could go to town to sell their wares and tell fortunes.

The Roma considered several factors when choosing a campsite. The first, and most important, was the proximity to good grazing land for their horses. Being near to a stream was essential, as was finding fairly dry ground so that their wagons did not get mired down in the mud. The Roma also sought out isolated areas so that there was less risk of them being driven away by local authorities.

Horse-drawn caravans, in recent years, have been replaced with motor homes, trucks, and trailers.

The Non-Roma

Wherever and however they have traveled, the Roma have always chosen to live apart, fearing, among other things, corruption from the *gadje*. This fear of corruption has been especially strong in cases involving Gypsy children. The Roma's greatest concern throughout their history, however, has been that contact with the *gadje* would lead to the disintegration of their traditionally strong family and community ties.

The Roma also have been suspicious of the *gadje*, largely as a result of the persecution that has followed them throughout their history. The Roma, in response, have generally withdrawn from all unnecessary social and physical contact with the *gadje*.

Because of these fears and suspicions, most Gypsies greet the *gadje* with hostility and an unwelcoming attitude. To prevent problems from arising, the *Romaniya* includes many rules that regulate and restrict Roma relationships with the *gadje*. Outsiders are considered off-limits, marriage between the *gadje* and the Roma is forbidden, and anyone not of Roma origin is

The Scratching Scheme

In his book, *The Nazi Persecution of the Gypsies,* historian Guenter Lewy describes a method the Roma often used to obtain fresh food and meat. Called the Scratching Scheme, it usually involved young Gypsy children.

Several girls or boys would enter a food shop. Purposefully dirty and poorly dressed, the children would start scratching their heads pretending they had lice. The youngsters then proceeded to touch and examine various fresh food items. Horrified that the products might be contaminated, the butcher or grocer would often give the Roma children the meat or food rather than have it go to waste.

Occasionally Gypsy women participated in such schemes. They were aided in their tasks by the superstitions and fears of the villagers, who often gave them what they wanted for fear of the Gypsies casting spells on them.

considered *marime*, or having the potential to pollute and harm the Gypsy community.

Marime

The word *marime* refers to both the concept of pollution or uncleanliness and the banishment of an individual from the Roma community. This concept of untouchability or ritual pollution has an Indian origin, dating back to the use of the caste system in India and the group of people called "untouchables" who lived there. In India, the untouchables were considered the "lowest of the low" and have long been treated with contempt and disdain. To be in contact with such an individual was considered a threat, with the potential for evil, to the rest of society. So it is in Roma communities.

This belief in *marime* affects every aspect of Gypsy life from their preparation of food to their interaction with other people. Non-Roma have one of the strongest potentials to pollute, which is one reason why the Roma try to limit their interaction with outsiders. To break this unwritten code of *marime* regarding the *gadje* can mean expulsion from the Roma community.

Animals, with the exception of the horse which is highly respected among the Roma, are also a strong source of potential *marime*. Because of the animals' habits of licking their paws and bodies, the Roma have long considered dogs and cats unclean. Cats, in particular, are to be avoided at all cost. In many Roma communities, a purification ceremony is required if a cat so much as enters a house or trailer. This usually involves destroying anything the animal touched or, at the very minimum, a deep scrubbing of contaminated surfaces. Dogs are occasionally kept, not as pets but as watchdogs that are never allowed inside.

Cleanliness

Many of the traditional laws of *marime* involve water, as cleanliness is very important to the Roma. The Roma, for example, take only showers; they consider bathwater to be stagnant and unclean, and therefore *marime*. In addition, a towel used to dry the lower half of the body cannot be used for the top half.

Even indoor toilets are considered unsanitary. Many rural Roma still insist on going into the forest or bushes to expel their waste. Urban Gypsies, on the other hand, often post a guard at the bathroom door to make sure that no member of the opposite sex enters while someone is using the toilet.

The Roma also have very strict rules for using the water out of a stream or river. The water from the farthest point upstream

The Roma have many rules regarding personal cleanliness. A Gypsy woman scrubs her laundry.

is considered the cleanest and is used only for drinking and cooking. From that point and working downstream, the order of use for the water is as follows: bathing and washing dishes, washing or nourishing horses, washing clothes, and washing the clothes of a pregnant or menstruating woman. Separate bars of soap and separate pails are used at each location.

The Roma continue many of these practices in the twenty-first century. It is still considered improper, for instance, to clean eating utensils in the same sink or basin where humans wash. Men's and women's clothing are also washed separately.

Women as Marime

Women are greatly feared in Roma society because of their ability to "pollute." The Gypsies believe that a woman's body is divided into two parts: above and below the waist. Her upper body is considered clean, while the lower half is said to be *marime*. The reason for this belief is that menstruation is seen as shameful and unclean in Roma society. "The fact that blood flows without injury," write historians, "seems to be the proof of bodily impurity."[11]

The concept of a woman being *marime* results in very strict rules and taboos affecting what a woman can and cannot do. A Roma woman, for example, is required to wear a long skirt that covers her legs. The bottom of her skirt must never touch a man other than her husband. If for some reason a woman is not wearing a long skirt, not uncommon in Roma society today, she still must cover her legs with a blanket or coat when sitting down. If these rules are not followed and some portion of the woman's clothing touches a man, according to historian Isabel Fonseca, "this action makes him ritually unclean and in need of purification before other Gypsies can again associate with him."[12]

Breaking any of the *marime* laws can result in disciplinary action. When this happens, the parties involved appear before the *Kris*.

The Kris

The *Kris* is the Romani Tribunal, a kind of internal court that is responsible for dealing with problems within the Gypsy community. It has its origins in a similar kind of court system in India called the *panchayat*. The *Kris* is the ultimate power in Roma society and makes its decisions based on strict traditions and moral standards handed down through the generations. In speaking of Roma law, historians write: "Its main purpose is to achieve a state of balance or *kintala* that pleases the spirits of the ancestors."[13]

The members of the *Kris* are chosen on the basis of their wisdom and experience. Only men are included. Participation by the audience is also expected. Members of the audience, for instance, are allowed to ask questions of the witnesses, and when they feel the answers to be untruthful, audience members often hiss, laugh, or make jokes.

The charges heard by this court can include anything from the violation of mar-

Because Roma society believes that women are impure, it imposes harsh restrictions on their behavior.

riage vows to murder. No lawyers are present; the defendant and the plaintiff must represent themselves. Ultimately, however, it is the judges who make the final rulings.

Over the years, the Roma have had great success in refining their laws to adapt to the current customs of each country in which they lived. In addition, according to historians: "The Roma legal system not only protects the Roma from external and internal threats but also serves as a code that organizes Roma society."[14]

Punishments

Penalties for a guilty verdict range from the payment of court costs to the permanent banishment of a guilty individual from the Roma community. The decision of the *Kris* is always final. Even in the twenty-first century and subject to various state and national laws, the Roma do not consider the verdicts handed down by *gadje* courts to be final. A *Kris* will still be held among the Roma to mete out appropriate punishments within the Roma community. The Roma, however, at least in

Animal Training

Touring bands of Roma with trained dancing bears at one time provided entertainment in remote European and Russian villages. The bear acts were often part of Roma traveling shows and circuses that performed throughout the region. According to historian Isabel Fonseca in her book, *Bury Me Standing: The Gypsies and Their Journeys:* "Animal dancing is now dying out from a combination of pressure for animals' rights and loss of interest." The Roma and their dancing bears, however, can still occasionally be found performing in remote areas of the world.

The Roma have also been skilled horse trainers. The horse traditionally has been the most important animal in Gypsy society because of its significance in Roma mobility and survival. During their early years in Europe, the Roma became expert horse trainers and traders. They also possessed great skill in the art of curing and treating sick animals. It was not uncommon throughout Europe for the non-Roma to seek out the help of Gypsy horse trainers when their animals were sick, rather than rely on poorly trained veterinarians.

The Roma's interest and expertise with horses continues in modern Roma society. Many Roma today own horse farms where they breed and train horses to be circus performers.

today's world, usually abide by state or federal court proceedings in terms of payment of fines and prison sentences.

Once a sentence has been handed down by the *Kris*, it then becomes the responsibility of the entire Roma community to enforce any punishment. There are no prisons or jails within the Roma community, nor are there any police or law enforcement personnel. The Roma believe that peer pressure alone is sufficient to ensure adherence to the law and the judgments of the *Kris*. According to Solsten and McClure: "Disapproval or punishment by the community was [and is] a much more serious reprimand to a Gypsy than any legal action by the state."[15]

Marime or banishment from the community is the harshest penalty handed down by the *Kris*. The offenders in such cases are prohibited from having any contact with other members of the community. They are condemned to live in the world of the non-Roma. In addition to the punishment handed down to individual offenders, in many cases their families are also declared *marime* and ordered to leave the community.

A *marime* label can be removed only by the forgiveness of the offended party or by the passage of time. Readmission to Roma society is always a cause for celebration, but there is also a stigma attached to such individuals for the rest of their lives.

Stealing and Begging

Historically, the Roma have seldom turned to the non-Roma legal system for the resolution of a problem, while the non-Roma population has accused and punished the Gypsies for many crimes. These charges have ranged from murder and kidnapping to the more common crimes of begging and stealing. These latter charges were often true.

The Roma, in many cases, resort to begging and stealing to keep from starving. Historian Guenter Lewy explains: "Unable to obtain land and having no fixed abode, Gypsies had to rely on begging. Forbidden to do business with shopkeepers, the Roma have had to rely upon subsistence theft to feed their families."[16]

Historians Solsten and McClure agree. They write: "When food or money were needed, the Gypsy code permitted, as a last resort, stealing from wealthier people."[17] Because of this, many Gypsies do not consider stealing a crime as long as it is from the non-Roma.

The Roma at times also justify this stealing from the *gadje* by quoting an ancient Gypsy legend. Guenter Lewy explains: "Before the crucifixion of Jesus, a Gypsy stole the fourth nail, intended for Jesus' heart. In gratitude God gave the Gypsies a heavenly license to steal from the gadje."[18]

The Roma have also been accused of lying to the non-Roma. Because of their deep-seated suspicion of the *gadje*, many Gypsies consider lying to be a perfectly acceptable behavior. Isabel Fonseca explains: "Disinforming inquisitive gadje has a long tradition. It is a serious self-preserving code that their customs and language should not be made known to outsiders."[19] Hence, to lie to a *gadje* carries no stigma of wrongdoing.

Traditional Roma Occupations

While labeled as thieves and beggars and sometimes forced to fall back on these behaviors, the majority of Gypsies prefer to obtain what they need through some kind of employment. Their attitude toward work and saving, however, differ from that of many mainstream groups. According to Solsten and McClure, "They generally aimed at earning [only] enough to meet the needs of the day."[20] As a result, the Roma traditionally shun regular work hours and wages in favor of more independent and flexible kinds of labor.

Nomadism also has played a large role in determining the kinds of occupations available to the Roma. Because of their seasonal movement, they are forced to find work that can be done while traveling. For that reason, the Gypsies never took an interest in farming or the raising of crops. Nor have they been fishermen or hunters. Also, the Roma have to find work that involves little or no contact with the *gadje* in order to follow the rules of the *Romaniya*.

The Roma, when they first arrived in Europe, relied on a skill for which they were greatly respected and appreciated—metalworking. The Gypsies learned this ancient art in India and passed down the skills through the generations. Over the last five hundred years, they have made nails, tools, weapons, kitchen equipment, and a variety of other products. They are also expert jewelry engravers.

Gypsy vendors have always been and continue to be a common sight near their encampments and settlements. The Roma often set up small booths and sell their wares to passersby and occasionally sell door-to-door. The articles sold are usually of little value, the most common being baskets, brooms, combs, and wooden spoons.

Fortune-Telling

The Roma also have always been associated with fortune-telling. While never using this tradition among themselves, one of the most familiar images of the Roma is that of the Gypsy fortune-teller.

There were many reasons the Roma chose this occupation. In the first place, it gave them an aura of mystery and magic. This sense of mystery was useful to them in their dealings with the non-Roma world. During the Middle Ages (800–1500) in particular, the beliefs in magic and sorcery were common throughout Europe. The Roma's alleged ability to cast spells and predict the future sent waves of fear through superstitious Europeans. Fortune-telling was also an excellent way to earn money.

Gypsies display yarn for sale in Romania.

Telling Fortunes

To please their clients, most Gypsy women predicted favorable fortunes—that a young, lonely girl, for instance, would find a rich and handsome husband. On other occasions the Roma might use mysterious warnings of peril in order to frighten their customers. They would tell the fearful person that this misfortune could be avoided by using a certain herb or potion the Gypsy would then sell to the gullible client.

There were numerous devices and gimmicks the Roma used to tell fortunes. Throughout the years, Roma women have read tea leaves, seen visions in crystal balls, and even read cards in order to predict the future. In Iran, Gypsies sometimes used beans or the knucklebones of sheep. The most frequently used method, however, was palmistry. The Roma read meaning into the shape of the hands and fingers and the designs of certain lines on the palms.

Roma women still pursue this traditional occupation. Today Gypsy fortune-tellers can be found in carnivals and circuses around the world.

A fifteenth-century painting depicts a Gypsy woman reading a palm. The fortune-telling tradition of the Roma continues to this day.

Even the Roma admit that much of their fortune-telling skills are something of a hoax. For the most part, Gypsy fortune-tellers, who are always women, take advantage of the fears of the people with whom they come in contact. While claiming that their powers to predict the future come from God, in reality the real skill of the Roma lies in their ability to judge human character.

Over their thousand-year history, the *Romaniya* has guided the Roma in every aspect of their everyday lives. From the concept of *marime* to the practice of traditional occupations, the Roma know what is expected of them. These guidelines help the Roma to survive in a hostile world. They also serve them well in maintaining close families and communities.

Chapter 2

Roma Family and Community

The Roma way of life has always centered around family and community. Individual achievement means little; rather, the emphasis is on a strong sense of group identity and loyalty. As well as in every other area of their life, the Roma have very specific and strict rules that regulate family and community life. One of the many unwritten codes of the Roma, for instance, is their law of hospitality. It is the obligation of any and all Gypsies to offer welcome and help to any other Roma who ask for it. Deviating from any of these rules can lead to punishment or banishment from the group.

Roma Groups

Family or blood ties are the most important ones in Roma society. Large extended families characterize Roma society and it is common for grandparents, children, and grandchildren to all live in the same household. The extended family is referred to as *familiya.*

The Roma also place great importance on the clan, called the *vista* in Gypsy society. All members of the *vista* are related to each other with at least one ancestor in common. Each clan is ruled by a chief, called a *Rom baro* or *vaida,* meaning "Big Man." The *baro* is chosen for his age, experience, and wisdom and he is responsible for settling minor disputes within the group.

Occasionally clan leaders will adopt the name of "king" or "emperor." There is no true royalty or nobility among the Gypsies, however, so such names are generally bestowed only as a sign of respect. They do not necessarily signify political leadership or position within the community. The Roma did use imaginative titles of nobility such as duke and count when they first came to Europe, but these had no real significance and were meant only to impress the host country's leaders.

"Gypsies, themselves," writes Isabel Fonseca, "have never recognized kings. Local . . . leaders were the most any group needed or tolerated, and these men were really judges rather than rulers.

Communication

Throughout their history the Roma have placed great emphasis on maintaining contact with other clans and families. In the days before modern communication devices, the Roma had a remarkable and effective method of keeping in touch with one another.

A trail of messages in code, called *vurma*, was left along the roadsides of the countries through which the Roma passed. These messages took the form of twigs, bits of glass, bones, colored threads, and scraps of cloth. Only the Roma knew where to look for these items and what they meant.

This system is still used occasionally in rural areas of the world. More often, however, the Roma today make use of modern communication equipment. While few Roma communities have phone service, they nonetheless manage to stay in touch with one another over vast distances. The Roma use various contact points in cafes, bars, and grocery stores. In these places, the Roma receive mail and telephone calls. Whenever an emergency arises, such as the illness or death of a relative, the Roma have an uncanny and amazing ability to find one another.

Such leaders lasted only so long as they were respected."[21]

The other division within the Roma community is the *kumpania*. This is an alliance of households in the same geographic area that are bound together, not by family ties but by their need to earn a living. These groups are usually from ten to one hundred families.

Marriage

All Roma are expected to marry and have children so that the family and clan can continue to grow and remain vital. Marriages, throughout the years and in modern Roma society as well, generally occur at an early age, usually between the ages of nine and fourteen for both girls and boys.

Marriages between relatives, even distant ones, are forbidden in Roma society. The Roma, however, are expected to marry someone from their own ethnic group. In the past, marriage with a non-Roma usually resulted in an individual's exclusion from the community. Roma law occasionally allowed a Roma male to marry a *gadje,* but only if his non-Roma wife agreed to adopt the Romani way of life. This leniency did not extend to a Gypsy woman's marriage outside the group.

Bachelorhood is held in contempt and considered an unnatural state among the Roma. Until he is married, for instance, even if he is fifty years old, a male Gypsy cannot be called a Rom. In the same vein, a childless woman in Roma society is not considered an adult female.

In a similar fashion, there is no real concept of loneliness within the Roma community. "This conception of a lone person," writes Fonseca, "was invariably a Rom who, for some infraction, had been recognized as marime and had been excluded from the group. There was something wrong with you, some shame, if you had to be alone."[22]

Premarriage Rituals

In many parts of the world today, Roma make their own decisions about whom to date and marry. Parents might be consulted but the overall wedding plans are made by the young couple. Traditionally, this was not true, and in a few Roma communities today, tradition prevails.

The choosing of a bride was an essential and important duty for the parents of each young man. These arranged marriages often centered around a desire to create an alliance between certain families in the community. The young man's family carefully considered all the young

unmarried women in the community by evaluating each girl's individual qualities.

Physical appearance played only a small role in this decision. "The prospective brides are [instead] judged on their merits," write historians, "such as health, stamina, strength, disposition, manners,

A Roma couple poses on their wagon with their children. Marriage, a virtual requirement in Roma society, ensures the growth and vitality of the Gypsy community.

and domestic skills. The character of the girl's family, as well as their prestige in the community was also taken into account."[23]

The most important task during this premarriage period was the determination of a suitable bride-price. The bride-price was a payment of money, goods, or services, made by the groom's family to the family of the bride. Its purpose was to compensate the bride's parents for the loss of their daughter and her future earnings.

Once both parties agreed to an equitable price, the agreement was sealed with the father of the future bride drinking a symbolic glass of wine. Following this ritual, a ceremony called a *pliashka* was held for the family and friends of the engaged couple. In many cases this was the first time the bride and groom actually met each other.

"The symbol of this celebration is a bottle of wine or brandy wrapped in a brightly colored silk handkerchief, brought to the ceremony by the young man's father," write historians. "A necklace of gold coins is traditionally attached to the bottle. The groom-to-be's father takes the necklace of coins and puts it around the . . . girl's neck and warmly embraces his future daughter-in-law."[24]

This necklace made it clear to everyone that the girl was no longer available to other young men. After the groom's father drank from the wine bottle, he passed it around until it was empty. The bottle would later be refilled with wine or brandy and used at the wedding celebration.

The Wedding

The actual wedding or *abiav* is still largely a symbolic act within the Roma community. It has little religious or legal significance. The Roma believe that two people agreeing to live together is more binding than any actual service in front of a minister or other authority figure. Many Roma today still marry in this traditional way, but most also have a civil or religious ceremony to conform to the legal customs of the country in which they live.

In a traditional ceremony, a Roma couple simply join hands in front of a tribal elder and promise to be true to one another. In some Roma clans, the couple might jump over a broomstick together to symbolize a new stage in their lives.

Their vows to each other also can be sealed in several rituals using bread. In many communities, the bride and groom place a drop of their blood on a piece of bread and then eat each other's bread. In another ritual, a small amount of salt and bread are placed on the knees of the bride. The groom takes some of the bread, puts salt on it, and eats it. The bride does the same. "The union of salt and bread," according to the Roma, "symbolizes a harmonious future together."[25]

When the marriage celebrations and festivities are over, and before the couple leave for the night, another ritual takes place. The bride's family, with much weeping, kissing, and hugging, unbraid their daughter's hair as a symbol of her new marital status. Her new mother-in-law

A Roma couple dances during the celebration following their marriage ceremony.

then places a colorful head scarf, called a *diklo,* on the bride's head. This signifies her status as a married woman. She will never again be seen in public unless she is wearing this scarf.

Married Life

The Roma expect all couples to remain faithful to each other until death. Historically, infidelity has had serious consequences, particularly for a Gypsy wife. These consequences can include the woman's banishment from the community, but more typically the wife is simply returned to her parents, who are then required to return the bride-price. In cases of divorce, the tribunal or *Kris* determines how much of the bride-price needs to be returned. A girl's father also can remove his daughter from a marriage if he feels she has been mistreated.

Until the new couple has a child, they usually live in the same caravan, trailer, or house with the groom's parents. His mother is the matriarch or "head" of the family, and it is her responsibility to guide they are finally permitted to call each other husband and wife.

The Period of Pregnancy

Abortion and birth control are virtually unheard of within the Roma community. Instead, a couple's responsibility in life is to have children. Large families with eight to ten children are common. Children, the Roma believe, ensure the continuation of the family line and add respect to the family. Large families also have helped the Roma to survive and replenish their numbers after the exterminations of entire Roma populations, especially after World War II and the Holocaust.

The birth of a child is a special event in a Roma community. As in all other aspects of Roma life, the *Romaniya* requires that certain customs and rituals be followed during and after the birth process. These rites, the Roma believe, are needed to ensure a healthy and happy child. From the time a woman discovers she is pregnant until the infant's baptism several weeks after birth, these strict rules must be followed. The rules are based on the Roma belief that a woman is impure or *marime* during pregnancy and that the child is also unclean until he or she is ritually purified.

For that reason, during her pregnancy a Roma woman must be isolated from the

Gypsy couples are expected to remain faithful to each other. Consequences for infidelity are sometimes severe.

and control her daughters-in-law, called *boria.* A girl married to the eldest son in a family holds the highest position of honor in this extended family. It is not until a new couple become parents that they are permitted by Roma law to move into a home of their own. It is at this time that rest of the community. Because of her "impurity" only other women can come in contact with her. Even the woman's husband can visit for only brief periods of time. In addition, any object touched by a pregnant woman, either during pregnancy or in the period immediately following birth, must be destroyed.

The Birth Process

In the past the majority of Gypsy children were born in fields, forests, and haystacks. If the birth occurred in the family's caravan, the horse-drawn home had to be destroyed. Even today among both the nomadic Roma and those who are settled in permanent homes, the actual birth process occurs outside the family dwelling. A tent might be erected, a trailer might be used, or even another house might be selected for the duration of the pregnancy. This tradition continues, although many Roma women today choose to give birth in hospitals to prevent any danger of pollution to the family and community.

Male Domination and the Division of Labor in Roma Society

The world of the Roma is very male-dominated. Under Roma law a wife is considered subordinate to her husband, and she is expected to demonstrate this subservience in public. A woman must never walk in front of a man or even between two men while indoors. And at meals women are responsible for serving all male family members. They must do this from behind the men's chairs, and never while facing them.

In general, Roma occupations have been and still are divided according to sex. Men are usually the artisans and craftsmen while women offer services such as fortune-telling and housekeeping. Traditionally, it has been the women who usually brought in the largest amount of money. It also has been the women who performed the majority of work at home.

Even in modern times, the work hours for Roma women remain long. They often toil from dawn to dusk, performing a myriad of different tasks without the help of modern conveniences found in mainstream homes. For example, clothes washing is still often done by hand in tubs that are set up in large outdoor courtyards.

Many families still live with the husband's mother who dominates the family and assigns the tasks for each workday. Whether living in caravans or in more permanent dwellings, each daughter-in-law has her own set of chores and duties that must be completed before going to bed.

In traditional Roma communities, midwives—special female clan members who have experience with delivering babies—assist in the birth process. Certain rites are carried out immediately prior to delivery. "One rite among some tribes," write historians, "involves the untying of certain knots so that the umbilical cord will not be knotted."[26] In most cases this ritual involves the removal of all knots in the mother's hair and clothing. In many Eastern European countries the Roma also cover all windows with fabric to prevent anyone from seeing the newborn prior to baptism.

"The baby's birth was followed by lengthy rubbings in home-brewed unguents and sprinklings of a saffron-yellow, acrid powder,"[27] writes Isabel Fonseca, who observed a birth while staying with a Roma family in Albania. According to Roma belief, this is done in order to strengthen the infant and protect it from evil spirits.

Following these applications, the infant is wrapped in cloth, while pins and special talismans are pinned to the infant's gown or other clothing to further ward off potential evil spirits. Red thread often is tucked in to ensure good health and happiness. The Roma believe that the color red is a powerful force in helping to keep evil spirits away.

Infancy and Baptism

In addition to the rituals performed at birth, there are others that must be followed in the days and weeks afterward in order to ensure a healthy child. The first ritual is usually the formal recognition of a child by its father. In some Roma communities this is a simple matter of wrapping the baby in clothing belonging to him. It is traditional in other tribes, however, "for the mother to put the infant on the ground," write historians. "The father picks up the infant and places a red string around its neck, thereby acknowledging that the child is his."[28]

Roma children are baptized within a few weeks to a few months after birth. Until this time the mother and child remain isolated from the remainder of the community. Also, until baptism, the child's name cannot be said aloud and photographs of the infant are strictly prohibited.

Baptism involves the immersing of the infant in water in order to wash away any impurities. In traditional Roma communities, this ritual is done in a running stream. Following the immersion, the child is massaged frequently with special oils. The Roma believe it is at this time that the child actually becomes human.

Typically, a Roma child will be given three names. Only the baby's mother knows the first name and will forever keep it a secret. The Roma believe that this secret name will protect the child and keep his or her true identity from harmful supernatural spirits.

The child's second name will be used only among the Roma themselves. The third name is one that has little importance to the Roma. This name will be used when dealing with the non-Roma.

Roma Food

The eating habits of the Roma have also been influenced by their nomadic way of life. Their diet, for the most part, consisted largely of what was readily available in the countryside. Wild fruit, berries, leafy plants, and small mammals formed the bulk of their diet.

A favorite traditional Roma dish in Europe is hedgehog, known elsewhere as porcupine. Ideally, this animal is flavored with garlic, the favorite seasoning of the Roma, and placed intact, skin, quills, and all, above burning hot coals or stones in a pit. In this way, it is cooked in its own juices and is reported to have a pork-like taste.

Enormous quantities of food and drink are served at ceremonial events such as baptisms, marriages, and religious festivals. Daily meals for the Roma, however, are a different matter. The staple of the Roma diet has always been strong black coffee, a beverage that is consumed throughout the day. The Roma usu-ally eat their main meal around sunset. The basis of this meal is usually a thick, fatty vegetable soup or stew containing whatever local vegetables are available.

In recent years, those Roma who have had the most interactions with non-Roma society have adopted many of mainstream society's eating habits. This includes the use of fast foods, canned items, and bottled beverages.

Prepared here in a long-handled container, strong black coffee is prized among the Roma.

A Child's Life

It is the responsibility of everyone in the extended family and community to help raise a Roma child. Most children learn their roles in life by imitating their mothers and fathers, and then by helping them with the chores of daily life. The difficulties of a nomadic life have, over the years, served to toughen Gypsy children, who had to learn early in life to entertain themselves. As a result, the children learned to play with whatever items were available. Sticks and stones became weapons for Roma boys, while corncobs often became dolls for the girls.

Life on the road left little time for Roma parents to engage in play with their children. Even in modern Roma society, mothers and fathers have tasks that require their attention throughout the day. To an outsider, in fact, Roma parents often appear to be neglectful and rough in their treatment of children. According to an authority on Gypsies, Isabel Fonseca: "Gypsies were rough with their children (not their babies); or so I felt. They were always shooing them away, yelling at them, and smacking them, and the children didn't appear to be much bothered by any of it. It wasn't cruel or unusual; it wasn't frightening. Even play was rough."[29]

Hardworking Roma parents have little time to play with their children, who learn at a young age that they must amuse themselves.

Roma children are also taught at an early age that a clear-cut division exists between themselves and the non-Roma. The desirability of being a Rom is emphasized and they are encouraged not to socialize or have contact with the *gadje* unless absolutely necessary.

This need to remain separate from the non-Roma extends to Roma beliefs about formal schooling as well. American Gypsy Steve Tene talked of this idea during an interview with journalist Peter Maas in the 1970s. Maas writes: "Like most gypsy children, [Steve] was not allowed to attend school; nor did he have any social intercourse with non-Gypsies until he was twelve years old, when he finally fled from his family for the first time."[30]

Historians Eric Solsten and David E. McClure explain: "They [the Roma] see schooling as a hindrance to freedom."[31] While formal schooling was never deemed of great importance among the Gypsies of the past, the need for formal education is gaining wide support among the Roma of today.

Loyalty to family and community is one of the most defining characteristics of Roma society. Whether in the rituals of marriage or birth, the Roma live rich and fulfilling lives following the traditions handed down from one generation to the next. These traditions enabled the Roma to survive and adapt to changing conditions and to pass on their rich legacy to future generations. These rich traditions and customs also characterize the Roma's spiritual and artistic life.

Chapter 3

Spirituality and the Arts

The Roma do not have a religion of their own, nor do they have traditional priests and ministers. While many Roma today call themselves Muslim or Christian, few attend church or follow mainstream religious practices. "Though they have, for practical purposes, adopted the religions of those with whom they have come into contact," write Roma historians, "formal religion is often supplemented by faith in the supernatural, in omens, and curses."[32] In most cases the Roma prefer to carry out their religious ceremonies and rituals in their own homes and communities.

Historian Isabel Fonseca agrees: "Among themselves, they have no need of the religion of other nations. The Gypsies in Albania [for instance] do not have a religious life. It was [instead] a superstitious one . . . and their spiritual life consisted of a mixture of animism . . . and fear of ghostly ancestors . . ."[33] Animism refers to the belief that everything, including animals, forests, rivers, and even inanimate objects, possesses spirit or life.

Many Roma spiritual and religious ceremonies are accompanied by a rich and imaginative artistic tradition. No Roma funeral, for example, or other special occasion would be complete without the playing of sad and soulful Gypsy music. Roma musicians, from their roots in India to modern times, have entertained countless numbers of people with their songs and dances.

Basic Beliefs

While they have not adopted any mainstream religion as their own, the Roma have always believed in a supreme power or God. In Albania, for instance, many Gypsies are in the habit of adding the exclamation *ma-sha-llah* (as God wills) after many words and expressions. This statement reflects their belief that God is always with them and oversees their daily life.

The belief in the supernatural is also fundamental and universal among all Roma. They have faith in magic, in omens both good and bad, in powerful curses, and in miraculous cures. They also have a strong belief in invisible spirits, ghosts, and vampires who they believe reside in and haunt forests, rivers, and fields. The Roma believe that evil spirits exist everywhere and must be carefully guarded against and kept at bay through the use of spells and charms and by strict adherence to certain taboos.

An example of such a taboo is one that is carefully followed during the period immediately following the birth of a baby. A Roma husband, according to the *Romaniya*, is prohibited from visiting his wife and newborn child between sunset and sunrise. This taboo stems from the Roma belief that during this time, evil spirits, who lurk nearby during the darkest

Folklore

The Roma have a rich tradition of folklore and storytelling. Their legends and tales have been passed down orally through the ages and have entertained Roma children and adults for centuries. Specializing in ghost stories, fairy tales, and riddles, Roma stories are a rich combination of superstition and wisdom.

Author James Riordan recounts one such story in his book, *Russian Gypsy Tales:*

"Long ago there were three girls of marrying age in a Gypsy tribe. Their parents called on the village chief for advice. He summoned all the young men of the village and picked out the three that he thought would be most suitable for the young ladies. He told the men to go into the hills and bring back whatever each thought most necessary for life.

On the fourth day, the men returned. The first young man presented the chief with a lump of gold. 'You have spent your time wisely,' said the chief. 'That's a fine gift for a bride. You may marry the richest of these young ladies.'

The second young man presented the leader with the carcass of a deer. He was told that he was a fine hunter. 'Your family will never go hungry,' said the chief. 'You may marry the plumpest of the girls.'

Finally, the last young man stood before the leader. 'Well lad what is your gift? Your sack seems empty. Did you find nothing?'

The young man replied, 'I walked across the hills and saw such beautiful things. And I returned with this flower.' And the young man drew forth a most beautiful flower whose blossoms' light lit up the entire valley. 'Well then,' said the leader, 'since you can see beauty, you may marry the prettiest girl.' And the third young man gained the most beautiful girl in the tribe."

hours, might injure or imperil the unprotected baby.

To ward off such evil spirits, the Roma often resort to the wearing of good-luck charms and magic amulets. The Roma believe that such charms are imbued with magical powers that have the power to ward off danger. Furthermore, these items, the Roma believe, are sometimes able to heal the sick. These charms can take many forms, the most common being animal feet, special herbs, or even food items. One common practice, for instance, is carrying bread in a pocket to act as protection against bad luck.

Religious Pilgrimages

The Roma also believe in saints and the healing powers of certain sacred places. For hundreds of years, tens of thousands of Roma have gathered on the banks of the Rhone River at Saintes Maries de la Mer in France to pay homage to their patron saint, Black Sarah. Many of the Roma embrace and believe in the legend of Black Sarah, who, according to the Roma, was a maid to Jesus' aunts, Mary Salome and Mary Jacobe. The legend is that following Jesus' crucifixion, these two women and Black Sarah were cast out by the Romans into the open sea in a boat with no oars. The boat and its occupants eventually washed up on French shores.

Every May 24 the Roma gather at this site to celebrate this saint. A black statue, complete with a gold headpiece and a pink lace robe, stands in an arched stone crypt beneath the town church. The Roma pilgrims run their hands over her face and often leave shoes and other small offerings at her feet.

Each summer, thousands of Roma also journey from across Europe to the basilica at Lourdes, France. Lourdes has long been a famous pilgrimage site known for the large number of miraculous healings that have been reported there.

Beliefs About Illness

Roma belief in the supernatural is quite apparent in their traditions concerning sickness. The Roma believe that illness is an unnatural condition. They also believe that there are many supernatural ways to prevent or cure disease. These methods, while sometimes appearing ridiculous to non-Roma onlookers, are taken very seriously by the Roma and, in many cases, are still utilized by the Gypsies today.

One method of lowering a fever, for instance, is to shake a young tree. The Roma believe that in doing so, the fever can be transferred from the sick person's body to the tree. Another method to reduce fever is for an individual to drink special herbal drinks and potions. Other kinds of curative drinks contain parts of sheep, hedgehog, and other animals, dissolved in wine or brandy and consumed while a family member invokes a special spell.

Many Roma also believe that carrying a hedgehog's foot will prevent toothaches and that carrying a mole's foot can cure rheumatism. And, in Great Britain in the 1940s, according to Isabel Fonseca: "Gyp-

Gypsies march in Saintes Maries de la Mer in France in a procession honoring their patron saint, Black Sarah.

sies suffering from pulmonary [lung] disease attempted a symbolic transference [of the disease] by breathing three times into the mouth of a live fish, and then throwing it back into the stream. . . . The hope was that, confused, death would go for the fish."[34]

Even today, the Roma rarely use hospitals. "Among the Gypsies, a stay in the hospital," writes Fonseca, "for any reason other than giving birth could only mean death."[35] This has become a self-fulfilling

prophecy, as far too many of the Roma wait until someone is critically ill before calling on *gadje* physicians.

Beliefs About Death

The Roma are extremely superstitious about death. They believe that death is an unnatural occurrence caused by supernatural spirits or other unseen forces.

The Roma believe that there are many omens that herald the approach of a fatal illness or death. The most common omen

Roma Revivals

Massive revival meetings today play a significant role in the religious and spiritual life of the Roma. At one meeting held in France in 1998, over forty thousand Roma attended. Reporter Sarah Chayes attended this meeting and reported what she saw in National Public Radio broadcast of a documentary about Gypsies in 1998. She stated: "On either side of a mile-long runway, trailers stretch across the grass. Canopies are deployed, and cook stoves and plastic chairs sit out, forming each family's dining room." During the several-day revival meeting, different Roma elders and a few ordained Christian ministers took turns speaking to the large assembly.

This kind of revival also offers the Roma an opportunity to meet and interact with other Gypsies from around the world. Non-Roma townspeople, however, continue even today to treat the Roma with suspicion. Many of the shopkeepers board up their stores and leave town. Hundreds of riot police usually are called out to prevent violence between the two groups.

is the screeching or presence of an owl. When such an omen appears, "the vigilant," according to Fonseca, "would attempt to scare death away, perhaps literally by screaming at it, or by raising their skirts and flashing at it. They might try to trick death by changing the name of a sick person to that of someone they hated."[36]

The Roma believe in reincarnation, a belief that the soul of the dead will return in human or even animal form. There also is a great fear among the Roma that the dead might return in some supernatural form to haunt the living. Unless strict precautions are taken, this supernatural form, called a *mulo*, meaning the living dead, might escape from the dead body and take revenge on any individual who had harmed him or her while living. "It is for this reason," write historians, "that the body should not be touched, and that all objects that belonged to the dead must be destroyed."[37]

Caring for the Dying

When someone falls ill in a Roma community and death appears imminent, the Roma immediately send word to all relatives to return home. It is the family's responsibility, no matter how far away they live, to make every effort to travel to the bedside of the dying. This is necessary for two reasons. The first is simply to show family support and solidarity. The second, and more important, reason is the need for relatives to obtain forgiveness from the person who is dying. If a person dies while still harboring negative feelings or resentments, his or her spirit might return to inflict harm on the surviving offender.

There are many traditions and rules that must be followed during the last days of an individual. For instance, the dying Rom must never be left alone. Not only is this ritual followed in order to offer compassion and sympathy to the dying, but it is done to prevent the sick person from becoming angry that he or she has been left alone.

It is also imperative, for fear of contamination or *marime,* that the dying Rom not die in his or her home. During the period of time when the Roma were predominantly nomadic, family members usually moved the dying to a place located away from the tents or caravans. In those cases of sudden death when the individual did not have an opportunity to go elsewhere, the Roma community usually burned his or her tent or caravan. In modern times, however, a dying Rom might be sent to the hospital so that he or she does not die in the home.

The Death of a Rom

The Roma never touch a dead body out of fear of being contaminated. This is one of their strongest *marime* prohibitions. As a result, most of the dying are washed and dressed in their finest clothes in the days preceding the actual death. When this is not possible because of sudden death or other reasons, a non-Roma, usually an un-

dertaker, is called on to perform these tasks. "Some tribes may [even] plug the nostrils of the deceased with beeswax or pearls to prevent evil spirits from entering or leaving the body,"[38] scholars write.

All material ties with the deceased must be carefully and completely destroyed. Even the use of his or her name is avoided. Normally, clothing and linens are burned, while eating utensils, furniture, and jewelry often are destroyed or buried. Although this rule does not apply to horses, occasionally other animals owned by the deceased are also destroyed to prevent any possibility of *marime.* This custom of burning had its origins in India, where the Hindu continue to follow this tradition.

These rituals continue in Roma society in the twenty-first century. Today, however, amidst the poverty facing many Roma communities, most of the deceased's articles are sold to the non-Roma instead of being destroyed.

Mourning and Funeral Rituals

Like other facets of Roma life, the period of mourning following a death is governed by many rules and rituals. According to Roma sources, "There is a total absorption in the mourning, with no distractions or activities."[39] Between the time of death and the burial, for instance, Roma rules strictly forbid any survivors to wash, shave, or even comb their hair. No food is prepared or consumed. In addition, mirrors are usually covered while all vessels normally containing water are emptied.

In this 1958 photo, mourners burn a dead Gypsy and her belongings. The ritual exemplifies the Roma's fear of contamination from the dead.

A deceased Roma is usually buried with some of their possessions in order to ensure a good journey from this life to the next. These items can be almost anything, but most frequently include clothing articles, tools, eating utensils, money, and jewelry.

In the past, during their years of nomadism, the Roma often just left the dead behind at campsites and, occasionally, even on the roadway. Today, a huge funeral is more common. In many cases the family hires a small band to play Roma marches during the formal procession to the cemetery.

Many Roma communities have their own cemeteries. In other cases the dead are buried in church cemeteries, most often in a section far away from the non-Roma. These separate sections have been mandated by non-Roma church officials due to pressure from their congregations, who have demanded segregated cemeteries.

All along the funeral procession route and around the grave site, family and friends gather and vocally demonstrate their grief with loud sobs and crying. This display of sorrow reaches its peak as the coffin is lowered into the ground. Each family and community member is expected to throw soil or objects such as talismans and amulets on the coffin.

Most mourners in the Roma community wear either red, white, or black clothing. White in particular, the Roma believe, is a symbol of purity, protection, and good luck, while red and black offer protection against evil spirits.

Following the graveside service, a huge feast called a *pomana* is held. This is traditionally the first meal eaten by the mourners

Gypsies perform a musical tribute in a funeral procession. The Roma have long incorporated music into significant life events.

after the death of their loved one. These meals will be repeated at intervals of nine days, six weeks, six months, and one year. At each of these, certain relatives, beginning with the most distant ones, will announce their intentions of ending their mourning period. The final members to do so are the immediate family who end their mourning period at the one-year mark.

Music and Dance

No Roma funeral would be complete without the playing of moving and soulful Gypsy music. Their music, whether played at funerals, weddings, births, or baptisms, has always been a rich and imaginative part of Roma life.

When the Roma left India centuries ago, they carried with them a rich tradition of music and dance. As early as the fifteenth century, when they arrived in Europe, the Roma found employment as court musicians for the nobility of that continent. By the end of the eighteenth century, Roma orchestras were an established feature of eastern European entertainment. "Band members were often related," writes Hungarian Rom Dork Zygotian, "giving rise to family dynasties of Gypsy musicians which endure to this day . . . many of whom have branched into jazz, winning international recognition."[40]

In addition, early Roma musicians also played at banquets, special celebrations, and military events. According to the editors of *World Book:* "In the Austro-Hungarian army, Gypsy musicians played tunes called *verbunkos* to stir patriotic spirit."[41] The Roma later played music as Eastern European troops marched into battle in World War I.

Roma Musical Instruments

Professional Roma groups or *tarafs* traditionally have used many different kinds of musical instruments, including the violin, flute, guitar, dulcimer, cello, lute, cymbals, and accordion. The violin, among all of these, has played one of the most significant roles in Gypsy music. The Roma believe that the wood for the first violin came from the thick forests of Transylvania in Romania.

Modern Roma music has absorbed many influences over the years. In many cases, the Roma borrowed music from the different countries through which they passed, and then added their own flavor. Since the large majority of the Roma cannot read music, their musical skills are all the more remarkable.

Today, Roma musicians called *lautari* still travel from village to village in many countries performing at weddings, births, baptisms, and funerals. Violin players are called *ceterasi*. Their captivating and lively music continues to inspire many villagers to leap up and dance. In addition, Roma violinists strolling among diners in fancy restaurants have long been a common sight in parts of Europe and elsewhere.

Roma Dance

Dance also plays a prominent role in Roma society and is often breathtaking to watch. "The emotional power comes from

Django Reinhardt

The name of Django Reinhardt is well known to jazz lovers everywhere. From 1928 to 1953 Django recorded over one thousand songs. His influence on jazz music has been tremendous.

Born in a Gypsy caravan in 1910, Reinhardt lived most of his life in France. He grew up a wanderer, living on the road and traveling across Europe with his mother. He learned at an early age to play various musical instruments, including the violin, banjo, and guitar. It was this latter instrument that made him famous.

In his early teens, Django began playing with other Roma musicians in cafes, dancehalls, and nightclubs throughout France. He already had made quite a name for himself when tragedy struck. Severely burned in a fire in his caravan, Django suffered extensive damage to his hands. In the years ahead, using only a couple of fingers on his dominant hand, he retaught himself how to play the guitar.

He soon began recording American jazz music, adding his own interpretations and rhythms to make the music genuinely and uniquely his own. Django is quoted in the *Gypsy Jazz Website* article, "Django," as once saying: "Jazz attracted me because in it I found a formal perfection and instrumental precision that I admire in classical music, but which popular music doesn't have." He died of a stroke on May 15, 1953, at the age of forty-three.

Jazz musician Django Reinhardt (center) was born in a Gypsy caravan.

Spanish flamenco dancers perform before a group of British Gypsies. The Roma are famous for their skill in performing the dramatic flamenco.

within the performer who abandons him/herself to his/her art and breathes life into it," write Roma music historians. "The dances also represent freedom—freedom of personal and spiritual expression."[42] Their dance style often involves much hip shaking and body movement while they clap their hands above their heads.

The Roma are probably the most famous for a unique dancing style called the flamenco. Flamenco is the traditional song and dance of the Roma who settled in the Andalucia region of southern Spain. It developed over several centuries from Romani, Moorish, Andalusian, and other roots, becoming widely popular in the early nineteenth century.

Flamenco is still immensely popular today. Skillful footwork, finger snapping, and forceful but flowing arm movement characterize this powerful dance. The dancers are accompanied by guitar players, whose music is often so intense and lively that onlookers join in the entertainment, clapping their hands and shouting. Roma dancers, wearing colorful costumes, have long delighted audiences around the world.

As in every other aspect of their culture, the Roma follow many traditions in their spiritual and artistic lives. These practices allowed the Roma to maintain their way of life separate from the non-Roma for centuries. Even during the worst times of persecution and discrimination, their beliefs and practices gave strength to the Roma and enabled them to survive.

Chapter 4

The Early Years

The Roma have no written or oral history. Because of this, the first recorded evidence of their existence dates back to the early fifteenth century when they arrived in eastern and central Europe. Because of the lack of any earlier documentation, the origins of the Roma remained unknown until the late eighteenth century.

Origins

It was a Hungarian theology student, Stefan Valyi, studying at the University of Leiden in the Netherlands, who first considered the country of India as the possible ancestral homeland of the Roma. In 1763 Valyi met three students from India whose speech was quite similar to a number of Gypsies he knew. After that chance encounter, Valyi wrote an article that was later read by other scholars.

These scholars investigated Valyi's theory. During the next one hundred years, they analyzed every aspect of Romani, the language spoken by the Gypsies. It became increasingly clear to them that many Romani words were related to the Punjabi and Hindi languages of northwestern India.

Further research clearly established that the Roma were not descended from one specific group in India but several. Two of these groups were the Luri and the Dom. The Luri were a tribe of wandering minstrels, while the Dom had long been known in India as a nomadic tribe. Continuing their nomadic ways, other descendants of the Dom still exist in parts of India. Their occupations are quite similar to those of the Roma and include such jobs as basket making, music making, dancing, and scavenging. Like the Roma, they are well known as expert metalworkers.

The Roma can also trace some of their roots back to another group of people in India. Historians elaborate: "The Roma are descendants of the ancient warrior classes of northern India, particularly the Punjab, and they are identifiable by their language, religion, and customs which can be directly linked to those of the Punjabi of northern India."[43]

Migration to Europe

No one knows for sure why these different ancestors of the Roma left India. Historians, however, offer several theories. *National Geographic* journalist Bart McDowell writes: "Perhaps they were carried away by invaders, or left because of famines, social discontent, maybe even religious vows—no proof survived."[44]

Other scholars contend that the ancestors of the Roma were unhappy with their low social standing and left to find a better life. Most historians, however, now agree that the most likely reason for their migration was the invasion of Islamic troops from the west.

At the very beginning of the eleventh century, India came under attack by Muslim general Mahmud of Ghazni as he attempted to push the Islam faith eastward into India. Many thousands of people, including a group of Roma ancestors, fled this onslaught of foreign invaders.

Historians also theorize that there were several waves of migration from northern India. As the various peoples of Indian descent moved farther and farther away from their land of origin, they began to acquire their own distinct ethnic identity. It was at this time that the Roma came into their own as a people.

First Arrival in Europe

Historians have had an easier time tracing the Roma's route out of India. They have

Language

Today most Roma speak the language of the countries in which they live. Among themselves, however, many still speak their own native tongue, called Romani or Romany. Certain cultural events, such as the proceedings of the *Kris* and various ritual ceremonies, require the Romani language. The exclusive speaking of Romani also enables the Roma to maintain unity and cohesion among themselves.

Romani is a spoken language, not a written one. Each Roma clan speaks a unique dialect depending on where they live. The root language, however, is the same for all and is based on Sanskrit, the classical and literary language of the Hindus of India. Many Romani words are also related to the Punjabi and Hindi language of India.

The Romani language has also been deeply enriched by the borrowing of words from the languages of countries through which the Roma passed in their initial travels.

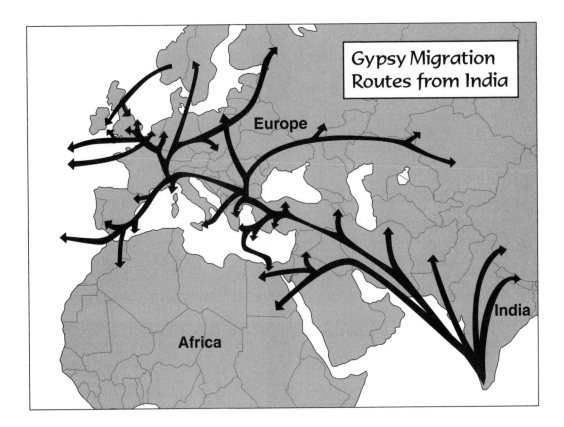

Gypsy Migration Routes from India

Europe

Africa

India

been able to do this by again studying the Romani language. By looking at certain words borrowed from other peoples, historians have determined that the Roma generally followed a route that took them from India to Afghanistan and then to Iran, Syria, northern Africa, and Greece. From there the Roma entered the Balkan region of Europe, which included such nations as Bulgaria, Romania, and Czechoslovakia. Many stayed in the Balkans, while others continued their migration into western Europe.

The Roma's estimated time of arrival in Europe differs from one historian to another. Some assert an arrival date as early as A.D. 1100, while others insist it was more likely during the early 1300s or 1400s. They nearly all agree that the people who would become the Roma left India sometime between the fifth and eleventh centuries.

Reaction of Europeans

At first the Roma were welcomed in Europe. In fact, historians often refer to the fifteenth century as the "Golden Age of the Roma in Europe." During this time they were warmly received by the aristocrats and monarchs of Europe, who gave the Roma letters of protection and also granted them other privileges.

An example of this kind of letter was issued to Gypsy Duke Ladislav on April 17, 1423, by King Zikmund of Czechoslovakia. In it, the king stated: "We recommend that you show to him the loyalty which you would show to us. Protect them, so that Duke Ladislav and his people may live without prejudice within your walls."[45]

The Roma presented this letter to French officials, were warmly greeted in that country, and were given the name *Les Bohemiens* in honor of one of the regions of Czechoslovakia named Bohemia from which they had come. This letter and others asked that kindness and generosity be shown the Roma. These letters were presented to officials in nearly every country of Europe.

The nobility of many European countries also admired the ironworking skills of the Roma. In fact, the rulers of Spain, Ferdinand and Isabella, used Roma-made weapons in the Spanish victory over the Moors in 1492. Roma skills also were appreciated by Bohemian king Vladislas (1471–1516) who used Rom metalworkers, according to historian David M. Crowe, "[for] the making of weapons and other warlike material."[46] Many Rom also served in the medieval armies of Europe.

Townspeople throughout the continent turned out by the hundreds to see the Roma during these first few years. According to writer Peter Maas, one reason for this turnout was curiosity. He writes that "not only because of their strange appearance and alien manners but also because the Gypsies had brought with them the arts of palmistry and fortune-telling."[47] Curiosity and appreciation for their skills, however, were soon replaced with more negative feelings.

An artist's depiction of a Gypsy in the fifteenth century, a period in which Europeans welcomed the intriguing Roma into their midst.

The Beginnings of Prejudice

The Roma entered Europe during a time of enormous social, political, and economic turmoil. Looking for someone to blame for their troubles, many Europeans focused their attention on the Roma newcomers. Since their arrival, "the Gypsies in Europe," writes scholar Ian Hancock, "have existed as a people without a geographical homeland, and without any kind of political, military, educational, or financial strength; an easy target for the application of blame."[48]

It was easy to blame the Roma. Because of their nomadic lifestyle, the Roma chose not to establish any permanent settlements, nor did they have any homeland to return to. In addition, being nonwhite, having an unfamiliar language, and dressing differently than the people of Europe, they were quickly and easily targeted as scapegoats, a group of people to blame for all the problems then occurring on the continent.

The initial curiosity and appreciation of the Roma soon disintegrated and turned into suspicion and fear. Dismissing the Roma's skills and colorful lifestyles, the people of Europe instead began to focus on the Gypsies as being lazy, dirty, disorderly, and dishonest. Within months of their arrival in medieval towns and villages, the Roma were often blamed for a variety of acts, including stealing, kidnapping, and prostitution.

Folklore historian James Riordan explains: "They [the Roma] were intruders, outcasts, who camped in pastures and meadows, paid no taxes, helped themselves to grain from the fields and sometimes robbed to survive."[49] The fact that the Roma's looks and actions were different from the majority population led to many accusations.

The Islamic Threat

The Roma were also associated with the Islamic or Turkish threat. At that time in European history, the Turks were a violent and aggressive people intent on spreading their religion into Europe. Historian David M. Crowe explains: "The unsettling and frightening Turkish conquest of the Balkans and the ongoing fear of Turkish incursions elsewhere intensified fear of outsiders, especially if they were dark skinned and non-Christian."[50] Although the Roma were not actually associated with the Turks, they were nevertheless feared and ostracized.

Ian Hancock agrees: "Association with the Islamic threat, their dark skin, and their various means to livelihood, which exploited the superstitious nature of the Medieval Europeans, all helped instill a negative image of the Gypsy in western traditions."[51] Charges of sorcery and witchcraft were made against Roma fortune-tellers, in particular. Their wild and often dire predictions spread fear and panic among the communities of Europe. The penalty for these charges was often death by burning.

The church, the controlling power in much of Europe, also mistook the Roma

Myths About the Origins of the Roma

While there is little doubt among historians today about the Roma's true origins in India, this was not the case in the past. Medieval Europeans, and even the Roma themselves, proposed several other theories.

Some Roma legends, for instance, assert that the Gypsies arrived in central Asia as early as the fifth century A.D., while other tales trace their roots back to the fourth century B.C. during the reign of Alexander the Great. Historians have been unable to substantiate either theory.

Among the Europeans, there have been suppositions that the Roma were among those who had survived the sinking of the legendary island of Atlantis. One of the most prevalent ancient superstitions, however, held that the Roma were the children of Satan. This charge helped lead to many negative stereotypes and also to the centuries of persecution by the various churches of Europe.

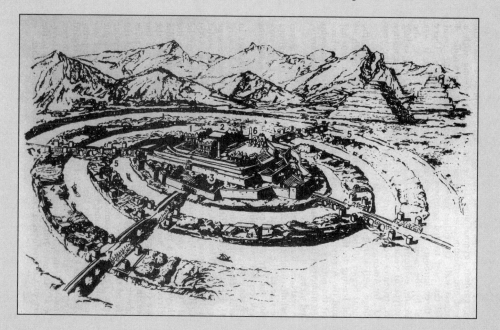

A fanciful illustration depicts the capital of the legendary island of Atlantis. Some Europeans believe the Roma originated on Atlantis.

A Gypsy places a curse on a gentleman who refuses to give her money. The church regarded the superstitious Gypsies as heretics.

for Turkish spies. In addition, the church saw heresy in the Roma's superstitious beliefs and their practice of fortune-telling. As early as 1427, the Archbishop of Paris excommunicated the Roma, calling them pagans and forbidding them to worship in mainstream churches. This attitude by the then dominant church in Europe greatly influenced the populace who increasingly began to view the Roma as a threat. The actions of the Archbishop of Paris were the beginning of four centuries of discrimination and persecution by the church and other authorities.

The Beginning of Roma Persecution

As a result of these suspicions and charges, the leaders and people of Europe decided that something should be done about what they perceived as the Roma threat. In the beginning years of persecution, the answer seemed to lie in the expulsion of the Roma from the different countries of Europe. When that tactic failed, Europeans turned to more repressive acts and violence. These actions would ultimately escalate and result in several attempts to actually exterminate the Roma population.

Rulers of individual countries, beginning in the fifteenth century and continuing to the present day, began to issue various decrees and edicts for the purpose of expelling the Roma from their territories. Historian Isabel Fonseca explains: "Between 1471 and 1637, the nation states [of Europe] threw themselves into a cooperative of cruelty . . . there was hanging and expulsion in England; branding and shaving of heads in France."[52]

These actions, officially sanctioned by the governments of Europe, were merely the first in a long series of discriminatory and persecutory moves made against the Roma. "The persecution of the Roma . . . belongs among the darkest pages of European history," historians write. "The Roma's life was never easy. They were always among the poorest population groups, and . . . Christian Europe never behaved towards them in a very Christian manner."[53]

Edicts and Decrees

Most of the edicts and decrees issued by European leaders spelled out the punishments that the Roma faced for failing to leave each country. France, for instance, enacted a series of laws against the Roma beginning in 1510. The French ordered that any Rom who failed to leave the country was to be flogged and whipped. Roma women might have their heads shaved and might also be sent to workhouses. Roma men, on the other hand, often were branded and put into chains and forced to serve on French ships.

In 1689 the kings of both Denmark and Sweden declared that any leader of a Roma tribe found on Danish or Swedish soil was to be sentenced to death. Gypsy hunts were organized by many government authorities throughout Europe. Rewards were offered for the capture or killing of any Gypsy. During these hunts, the Roma were hunted down like wild animals.

Signs were posted throughout the English countryside ordering the Roma to leave English soil. The Roma did not understand the English language, much less read it. This fact did not deter the English from putting captured Roms to death for their failure to obey the law. By the middle of the sixteenth century, it was even a crime for a non-Roma to offer any support or sympathy to the Roma.

French authorities enacted a law that forced the Roma to carry internal passports, called *carnet*, while traveling in that country. These documents required fingerprints and pages of often absurdly detailed information. Among the statistics required were chest measurements, the length of each finger, the size of the left foot and right ear, and the exact distance from the end of the middle finger to the elbow. These passports were required well into the twentieth century.

The Roma were also exposed to torture and bodily mutilation. In Moravia, for instance, the left ear was cut off all Roma women, while in Bohemia, the right ear was removed. "The greatest persecution in Czechoslovakia," write Roma historians, "came after 1697 when the Roma were placed by Imperial decree outside the law. Anyone could shoot, hang, or drown them, and killing the Roma wasn't considered a crime."[54]

French authorities check a Gypsy's internal passport. Roma traveling in France were required to carry documentation.

Slavery

In addition to the various decrees and punishments devised to repress them, thousands of Roma were also enslaved. In September 1445 Prince Vlad Dracul (Vlad the Devil) of Romania captured over ten thousand Gypsies while invading neighboring Bulgaria. He became the first European leader to import large numbers of Roma and enslave them.

By the end of the fifteenth century thousands of additional Roma had become slaves in Moldavia and Walachia, both part of present-day Romania. They were sold at slave auctions to Romanian noblemen who needed laborers to work on their vast landholdings and estates. The Roma also were used as slaves by the church and its clergy. Both groups forced the Roma to work under extremely harsh and brutal conditions.

Gypsy enslavement spanned four centuries. According to Fonseca, "Anyone who could not name his or her master when stopped on the road automatically became the property of the Crown."[55] This was true especially in the countries of Eastern Europe. The Roma's skills in metalworking made them indispensable to Eastern European monarchs and their economies. For centuries in Europe, the words "Gypsy" and "slave" were interchangeable.

During the colonial period, which continued from the sixteenth through the eighteenth centuries, many European nations dealt with the so-called Gypsy problem by sending large numbers of Roma overseas. In the 1700s Portugal became the first country to deport Roma slaves to their colonies in Africa, Brazil, and India. Other European countries soon followed. The French sent Gypsies to the Caribbean, while the Spanish shipped them to the Americas. The English and Dutch also were large exporters of Roma slaves, who were sent overseas to work on large plantations and landholdings in North America and the Caribbean.

The enslavement of the Roma continued until the year 1864, when the slave trade and slavery were abolished in Europe.

The Second Roma Migration

A second Roma migration occurred toward the end of the nineteenth century in the years immediately following the demise of slavery in Europe. Thousands of Roma took advantage of their newfound freedom to leave Europe for the Americas. Hoping to find employment, better living conditions, and less prejudice, the Roma began arriving in the United States in large numbers. Most came from Russia, Serbia, Hungary, and Romania.

Early Roma immigrants to the United States worked in many of their traditional occupations, most notably as metalworkers. They also developed a profitable fortune-telling business in America. Their hopes of a better life and less persecution, however, were quickly dashed. The Roma were greeted with the same suspicions and fears that had characterized their lives in Europe.

The first American account to discuss the Roma at any length appeared in the *Christian Enquirer* on September 29, 1855. This article stated: "The Gipsies . . . are an idle, miserable race, a curse to the countries they inhabit, and a terror to the farmer through whose lands they stroll. They seem utterly destitute of conscience, and boast of dishonesty as if it were a heavenly virtue. So deeply rooted are sin and vagrancy in the hearts of this miserable race, that neither penal laws, nor bitter persecution, can drive it out."[56]

Similar comments and opinions later appeared in a textbook, published in 1918, that was widely used in American law schools. "They are the living example of a whole race of criminals. . . . They will endure hunger and misery rather than submit to any continuous labor. . . . They murder in cold blood in order to rob."[57]

And in the 1911 edition of the *Encyclopedia Britannica:* "The Gypsies can, with some justification, be called parasites . . . the mental age of the average Gypsy is thought to be about that of a child of ten.

Early and Negative Stereotypes

For centuries the Roma have been cast as scapegoats and outcasts. They have been blamed for every sort of evil and crime. For many people, just the mention of the word Gypsy conjures up an image of dirty women in long skirts begging for money and telling fortunes.

The Roma were not always looked upon as even human. Many scholars over the years have included the word "nonhuman" in their definitions of the Roma and their way of life. Called pagans (people who believe in the supernatural and who are not Christian, Jewish, or Moslem), heathens, and worse, throughout their long history the Roma have had to contend with these negative stereotypes. These derogatory opinions have made it extremely difficult for the Roma to overcome their image as outsiders and outcasts.

The Roma also have been so associated with begging, stealing, and cheating that a word based on their name came into use in the English language. This word is "gyp" which means to swindle or cheat.

Misinformation, misconception, and erroneous stereotypes about the Roma are as prevalent today as they were six hundred years ago.

Gypsies have never accomplished anything of great significance."[58]

These opinions characterized the general atmosphere and beliefs that greeted new Roma immigrants arriving in the United States during the late nineteenth and early twentieth centuries. In response to public outcry and governmental concerns, the United States Congress began to pass stringent immigration policies in 1885 that would eventually exclude the Roma and other ethnic groups from admission to America. These restrictions were eventually relaxed after World War II to allow small numbers of Roma and other groups to enter the country.

Despite all attempts to expel, repress, and eliminate them in both Europe and the United States, the Roma endured and survived. Facing continual threats to their lives and way of life, the Roma relied on their strong loyalty to family and community and their ability to adapt to changing conditions. Little did they know, however, that their greatest challenge—and danger—lay just ahead.

Chapter 5

O Porraimos, The Holocaust and Its Aftermath

January 30, 1933, marked the beginning of one of the darkest periods in not only Roma history, but world history as well. It was on that day that Adolf Hitler became chancellor or prime minister of Germany. Hitler, an abusive and power-hungry dictator, would serve in that position until his death in 1945, toward the end of World War II.

Almost immediately, Hitler and his associates began to take steps that would lead to the invasion of neighboring countries, such as Czechoslovakia and Poland, and to what Hitler called the "purification of the German race." The invasions would ultimately lead to World War II, while Hitler's actions to create a "super race" would lead to what history books refer to as the Holocaust.

The Holocaust

Between 1933 and 1945, over six million people of Jewish descent were imprisoned in concentration camps, tortured, and eventually killed. The number of Roma deaths reached one and a half million, a fact that has largely been ignored by historians.

In actuality, the number of deaths for both groups probably reached far higher figures. Countless thousands of killings went unrecorded, having taken place in the fields, forests, and streets where people were frequently shot down without provocation. Historians believe that most Gypsies, in fact, never got as far as the concentration camps. Local police forces killed them.

The Roma call the Holocaust *O Porraimos*, the Great Devouring. In more recent years, the words "genocide" and "ethnic cleansing," meaning the methodical killing of an entire cultural or racial group of people, have been used to describe the killings that ultimately took place.

Persecution in Germany

When Adolf Hitler and the Nazis (National Socialist German Workers' Party)

The United States Holocaust Memorial Museum

The United States Holocaust Memorial Museum is an American monument to the millions of people who died during the Holocaust. It also provides a place for the study and interpretation of Holocaust history. The Museum was authorized by Congress in 1980 to be a permanent living memorial to all victims. Located in Washington, D.C., near the National Mall, the museum is the largest memorial anywhere in the world dedicated to the victims of Nazi persecution.

The Holocaust Learning Center at the museum offers information on the liberation of the concentration camps, the war crimes trial, the victims, and the extermination camps, among many other topics. The personal histories of thousands of victims are also documented there. Until very recently, however, the Roma were not represented among the victims honored.

That changed on April 14, 1994, when the museum held its first commemoration of Roma victims. That this event finally happened was largely due to the efforts of American-born Roma scholar, author, and activist Ian Hancock, who tirelessly lobbied for Roma representation at the museum. He was aided by the United States Romani Council. There are today a number of Roma on the museum's Board of Directors.

Various American states have smaller Holocaust memorials, while there are efforts being made in parts of Europe to create the same kind of living monuments.

came to power in Germany in 1933, several laws that discriminated against the Roma in that nation were already in existence. Germany had been passing persecutory edicts and decrees against the Roma for many centuries.

As early as 1725, writes historian Guenter Lewy, "King Frederick William I of Prussia ordered that Gypsies over eighteen, both male and female, be hanged without trial."[59] And in the early twentieth century, any individual over the age of sixteen who could not provide proof of regular work was placed in a workhouse for a period of two years.

"They [the Roma] were seen as asocial, a source of crime, culturally inferior, a foreign body within the nation," historians write. "During the 1920s the police established special offices to keep the Gypsies under constant surveillance."[60] In addition, many communities organized citizens' committees that worked toward the relocation of Gypsies to impoverished ghettos set well apart from the rest of the population.

These actions were the ongoing result of centuries of discrimination. Lewy elaborates: "In the late 19th and early 20th century," he writes, "alongside the view of the Gypsy as primitive but idyllic people . . . there now emerged a far less benevolent picture of the Gypsy—a racially inferior group whose presence in Germany jeopardized the purity of the Germanic race."[61]

The Superrace

Adolf Hitler supported this theory of the Roma being an inferior race but took it one step further in believing that all

Nazi leader Adolf Hitler (left center) considered all non-Germanic "races," including the Roma, to be inferior.

people, regardless of ethnic roots, were inferior to the Germanic "race," whom he referred to as the Aryans. In reality, the Aryans are people who share common Indo-Aryan language roots. Ironically, the Roma belong to this group of people. Hitler ignored these facts and redefined the word Aryan to suit his own needs. His version of the perfect "superrace" was made up of those individuals with fair skin, blonde hair, and blue eyes.

Hitler's list of outcasts included people of Jewish, Slavic, and Polish descent and the Roma. Hitler viewed these groups as being different in tradition and appearance from those he believed were pure-blooded Aryan. Therefore, according to Nazi Party policy, they were unfit to share in the new Germany and the new Europe that Hitler envisioned. These ethnic groups, Hitler believed, contaminated German life and culture and needed to be eliminated.

"Roaming the countryside in caravans, earning their living as musicians, peddlers and fortune tellers," historian Lewy reports, "the Gypsies and their elusive way of life represented an affront to Nazi ideas of social order, hard work, and racial purity."[62] Historian Harold Tanner agrees, writing that the Roma were viewed by the Nazis as "asocial, subhuman beings, and members of a lower race."[63]

Concentration Camps

Beginning in the late 1930s hundreds of thousands of targeted individuals were arrested, packed into crowded trains, and sent to a variety of concentration camps or prisons in Germany, Austria, Poland, and elsewhere. Few concentration camps existed anywhere that did not contain at least some Roma prisoners. The conditions in these camps were deplorable.

Upon arrival in the camps each person's head was shaved by Nazi guards, a practice that was aimed at depriving prisoners of their dignity. Each ethnic group was given a different colored triangle to wear on their prison uniforms to enable guards to easily identify a prisoner's race or group affiliation. The Roma wore a brown triangle. Most prisoners had little clothing and no shoes and were forced to sleep on stone floors without benefit of any kind of covering. In addition, prisoners were branded with a permanent marking, in the form of a number, usually tattooed on the wrist.

Many prisoners literally starved to death. Food was minimal. Breakfast often consisted of nothing more than a cup of bitter brown liquid that was called coffee. A thin soup made of turnips, water, and salt often was the only lunch provided and a piece of stale, moldy bread was the only supper most prisoners could hope for.

To make matters worse, the food often was purposefully oversalted. This extra salt caused the prisoners to complain of a constant and extreme thirst. The little water they were given, though, was often tainted with bacteria and fecal matter. Bad food and bad water led to a variety of uncomfortable and debilitating diseases. Hundreds of thousands of prisoners died as a result of these unspeakable conditions.

German soldiers supervise the transportation of prisoners to concentration camps.

Prisoners were also subjected to hard, backbreaking work, often completely pointless. One common task was to break up stones, which were then carried from one place to another and back again.

Medical Experiments

Medical experiments conducted on the inmates by Nazi doctors added to the nightmare of the concentration camps. The most notorious of these physicians was Dr. Josef Mengele, who was referred to by many prisoners, and later by historians, as "Dr. Death." Mengele literally had the power to choose who lived and who died. Among Mengele's favorite "subjects," historians report, were Roma children. He, according to journalists for the

Medical Practices—Sterilization

Sterilization is an operation performed on both men and women. During the surgery, an individual's reproductive organs are removed, thereby preventing any possibility of pregnancy in the future. The Roma, more so than any other ethnic group during the Holocaust, were victims of this particular practice. Thousands of Roma died during botched surgeries performed by underqualified Nazi physicians.

A small number of Roma men who agreed to this procedure were actually released from the concentration camps, but only if they agreed to serve in the German army. This release affected an insignificant portion of the Roma population and occurred late in World War II, at a time when the German army was desperate for troops.

Far more often, it was Roma women who were subjected to sterilization. This was definitely true during the years of the Holocaust. The use of sterilization, however, can be traced as far back as the Middle Ages when Gypsy women were forced to have this operation in accordance with the laws of many European countries.

As recently as 1972, a sterilization program was ordered in Czechoslovakia that called for this operation to be performed on Roma women who lived there. Czech authorities rationalized the operation by calling it an act of "socialistic humanity." Claims of a high rate of mental retardation among the Roma were made to justify this program, which continued well into the 1980s.

Economist, "liked to put out Gypsy children's eyes."[64]

The Nazis rationalized these various medical experiments by claiming they were intended merely to further prove the superiority of the German race. Calling the practices "medical research," the Nazi physicians conducted thousands of painful and brutal tests on the Roma and other ethnic groups.

In many concentration camps, for instance, "The Gypsies were injected with sea water," writes Isabel Fonseca, "to discover how long humans could survive in salt water."[65] These injections were usually lethal. In addition, on numerous occasions Roma prisoners were deliberately exposed to rare and fatal diseases so that Nazi doctors could experiment with various "cures." Again, most of these experiments resulted in painful deaths.

The Final Solution

In July 1938 Hitler and his associates finalized their plans for the *Endlœsung* or Final Solution. These plans called not only for the imprisonment of countless thousands of victims but the execution of hundreds of thousands of others. People of Jewish heritage were the primary targets, but not the only ones marked for death. Isabel Fonseca explains: "Under the Nazis, the Gypsies were the only group apart from the Jews who were slated for extermination on the grounds of race."[66]

Despite earlier imprisonments and executions, the actual proclamation calling for the specific extermination of the Roma did not come until July 1942 when Heinrich Himmler (1900–1945), the head of the Nazi police forces, announced: "The Gypsies are to be exterminated."[67]

Whether the German populace knew of these exterminations is a matter of debate that historians continue to struggle with today. The fact remains, however, that the majority of Europeans shared the Nazi view of the Roma as being members of a lower race. As historian Lewy points out: "When the Nazis intensified the harassment and persecution [of the Roma] . . . most of their [non-Roma] neighbors remained superbly indifferent. Worse . . . pressure for stepping up the harsh treatment meted out to the Gypsies came not only from the top Nazi leadership but also from the party's rank and file and from the German population itself."[68]

The Executions

In January 1940 the first mass execution of the Roma took place at Buchenwald, a concentration camp in Germany. This and other mass executions took place in what were called gas chambers, large rooms where sometimes hundreds of people were exposed to deadly gas fumes. According to scholar Ian Hancock: "250 Romani children were murdered in Buchenwald, where they were used as guinea pigs to test the efficacy of the Zyklon-B crystals, later used in the gas chambers."[69]

"The first mass murder of Gypsies in Auschwitz [a concentration camp in Poland] took place on March 22, 1943," writes historian Guenter Lewy. "On that day a group of about 1700 Gypsies—men, women and children—were taken to the gas chambers and killed."[70] Another such killing took place two months later.

Some sixteen thousand Roma were imprisoned at Auschwitz, one of the most notorious of the concentration camps used by the Nazis during World War II. The diary of Rudolf Hoss, Nazi commander of Auschwitz, reveals what happened to the Gypsies there: "In July 1942, the Reichsfuhrer SS [Heinrich Himmler] visited the gypsy camp. He saw those who were sick . . . the children. . . . He saw it all . . . and he ordered me to destroy them."[71]

A former Roma prisoner spoke of the treatment handed out to the Roma when he was interviewed by *National Geographic* journalist Bart McDowell about his memories of Dachau, another notorious concentration camp, located in Germany. "All Gypsies wore the prison uniform—stripes and a brown triangle upon the left breast and on their trousers. . . . Of the first 2000 [that arrived] I know of none who lived."[72]

Despondent Gypsies sit in an open area of an unknown concentration camp in 1945.

The Results of the Holocaust

It has been estimated that over half of the world's Roma population was killed during the years of the Holocaust. According to historians: "The number of deaths was large enough to tear apart the Gypsy society and leave them scattered, broken and utterly powerless. Unable to wield enough strength to speak for themselves, the obliteration of the Gypsy race seemed to fade away into forgotten history."[73]

In many countries entire Roma populations had been nearly eliminated. After the liberation of Czechoslovakia, for instance, only about six hundred Romani men and women returned to their homes. "The original Roma population in Czech lands was thus almost annihilated during the period of Nazi occupation,"[74] historians write.

That the Roma survived as an ethnic group is a testament to their courage and their ability to endure whatever hardships they encountered. In the years following World War II, the Roma retreated into their close-knit family groups and communities in order to regroup and gather what strength they still had. One factor that helped lead to the resurgence of their population was their long-held tradition of having large families.

The Nuremberg Trials

To make matters worse for the Roma, their massive losses and deplorable treatment were never addressed in the years following World War II, despite a number of well-publicized trials. The most famous of these was the one held at Nuremberg, Germany, that resulted in many Nazi leaders being found guilty of war crimes and eventually executed for their involvement in the Holocaust.

During these trials, called the Nuremberg War Crimes Trial, however, not one Roma was called as a witness by the Allied prosecutors. Isabel Fonseca elaborates: "Although sufficient documents were available . . . the mass murder of Roma . . . was not addressed at the Nuremberg Trials. To this day [1996] just one Nazi has received a sentence specifically for crimes against Gypsies."[75]

Reparations

The plight of the Roma has also been ignored in the years since the completion of the trials. During that time, the Roma, for instance, have received little, if any, financial reparations from any government for their loss and suffering. "The treatment of the Gypsies was certainly no less severe than that of Hitler's other victims," historians write. "However, less appreciation has been given for their suffering."[76]

"Only ten percent of the hundreds of millions of dollars made available by the United Nations for the survivors," writes Ian Hancock, "was set aside for non-Jews, and none of that found its way to the Romani survivors."[77] Western governments, including the United States, made little effort to help Roma survivors of the Holocaust.

Within the last twenty years, many Roma groups have begun speaking out and asking for financial compensation for their losses. The first steps toward the recognition of Roma persecution by the Nazis did not happen until the end of the twentieth century. In his acceptance speech for the Nobel Peace Prize in 1986, Professor Elie Wiesel (Jewish activist, Holocaust survivor, and author) stated: "I confess that I feel somewhat guilty towards our Romani friends. We have not done enough to listen to your voice of anguish. We have not done enough to make other people listen to your voice of sadness. I can promise you we shall do whatever we can from now on to listen better."[78]

Romania

Romania, often misrepresented as the homeland of the Roma because of the similarity in name, is home to the world's largest number of Roma. Around 2.3 million Roma live there.

Romania has been the focus of many superstitions and fantastic legends. It is supposedly the home of Dracula, whose legend originated in the forests of Transylvania. The countryside features dramatic castles, medieval towns, farms, and small villages.

Like the other countries of Eastern Europe following World War II, Romania fell under Communist control. It was one of the first countries, however, to rid itself of Soviet domination. In 1965, Nicolae Ceauşescu took control of the government during a wave of patriotism and furor over Soviet abuses.

Ceauşescu, a Communist himself, quickly became an even more abusive dictator than his predecessors. Greedy and corrupt, he instituted harsh policies that affected the Roma and many other ethnic groups. In 1989, however, he was overthrown and eventually executed. Romania became one of the new democracies of Eastern Europe.

With the increase in persecution that occurred during Ceauşescu's years and in the years following his overthrow, many Romanian Gypsies have since migrated elsewhere.

The Years Following the War

Any hopes the Roma may have had for an improvement in their status after the defeat of Adolf Hitler and Nazi Germany quickly faded. Conditions did not improve and the Roma, once again, were targeted as scapegoats.

Following the end of World War II, the Soviet Union and its army occupied much of eastern Europe. In country after country, elections were controlled so that the Communist Party would become the majority party and win control of the government. Calling these new governments "People's Republics," most were, in actuality, dictatorships run by the Soviet army and its leaders.

The Communists, like their Nazi predecessors, condemned the Roma for their failure to contribute to the new socialist states. Soon, the Roma were again being persecuted, this time under Communist rule, because of their nonconformist attitudes. In Bulgaria, for instance, Communist officials began to eliminate all Roma cultural organizations. Historian David M. Crowe writes: "The practical implication of these policies was the destruction of Roma self-identity through forced integration."[79] The same kinds of policies took hold throughout Eastern Europe.

A major part of the Communist governments' plans focused on Roma children. During the next twenty-five years, eastern European regimes ordered, often forcefully, the education of Roma children in public school systems. Unfortunately, these educational programs did not take into account the Roma's lack of language skills. Few Roma children could speak

Roma children learn to count in a makeshift classroom. For years after World War II, Communist regimes forced the Roma to send their children to public schools.

anything other than their own Romani language, nor could they read. These programs and others were ultimately dropped in the late 1970s when it became obvious that these efforts had failed.

In the years before, during, and after World War II, the Roma faced persecution and danger from many sources. Their numbers drastically reduced following the Holocaust, the Roma struggled to survive and preserve their rich traditions and way of life. Those tasks would face yet other challenges toward the end of the twentieth century.

Chapter 6

A Hostile World

The Roma have always lived in a hostile world among people who wanted to eliminate them. This is still true in places all around the world, but especially so in Eastern Europe. There, the persecution of the Roma has actually increased in recent years, especially since the fall of the Soviet Union and its satellite Communist regimes in the early years of the 1990s. "Treatment of the Roma," states Linda Wertheimer of National Public Radio, "has become Europe's most pressing civil rights issue."[80]

The End of Communism

The countries of Eastern Europe underwent a dramatic change in the late 1980s and early 1990s. One after another of the Communist regimes there were overthrown and eventually replaced by more democratic governments. This change to democracy, however, did not improve the Roma's status. "The most dramatic change for Central and Eastern European Gypsies since the revolutions of 1989," writes historian Isabel Fonseca, "has been the sharp escalation of hatred and violence directed at them."[81] Many European societies have singled out the Roma as scapegoats for the many hardships that these countries have faced in the difficult transition from Communist to democratic governments.

Historian David M. Crowe agrees: "Gypsies are now viewed as the symbol of all gone awry in the new democracies of Eastern Europe."[82] These feelings are compounded by the centuries-old fears and suspicions of the Roma that have characterized the general population's view since the arrival of the Roma in Europe in the fifteenth century.

As in the past, the Roma are innocent of the charge that they are responsible for the multitude of problems facing the new democracies today. That fact does not prevent the people of Eastern Europe from blaming them. Since the fall of communism, for instance, there have been dramatic increases in the crime rate in many countries. The public has, in large measure,

Violence in Western Europe

The violence against the Roma is not confined to Eastern Europe. Strong-arm tactics and violence also are becoming increasingly common in Great Britain. "*Spook Erection* is the name of a company that throws Gypsies out of their homes," reports Roma scholar and activist Ian Hancock in his book *The Pariah Syndrome.* "It is employed by several [town] councils. Spook's people are apt to use violence and intimidation, and there is disturbing evidence that Spook's methods are condoned by some local police and council officers."

In a small town in Great Britain, another incident led to the deaths of several Roma children in the late 1960s. In an effort to remove a Gypsy trailer from an area of town where the Roma were not wanted, a bulldozer was brought in to move the home. Inside was a young pregnant Roma woman, about to give birth, and her three young children. The family had refused to move until after the baby's birth. Ignoring the family's plea to wait, the bulldozer operator began to move the structure. In the process, a kerosene lamp was overturned. The ensuing fire killed the three children and resulted in the stillbirth of the child the Roma woman was in the process of delivering. No charges were brought against the bulldozer operator or company. The deaths were ruled as accidental.

tended to blame the Gypsies for this increase. "Gypsy youth, 18 years of age and younger," according to Crowe, "were accused of being involved in 44.2% of all criminal activity throughout Czechoslovakia."[83] In reality, Crowe says the percentage is well under 10%.

Efforts to Assimilate the Roma

The new democratic Eastern European governments have responded to the charges of Gypsy wrongdoing by attempting to integrate the Roma into mainstream society. The Communists had tried integration and failed as had many European leaders during the eighteenth and nineteenth centuries.

In 1761, for instance, Empress Maria Theresa of Austro-Hungary decided to turn the Roma into what she called "New Hungarians." The government gave the Roma tools, seeds, and animals and instructed them in farming techniques, despite the fact that never in their history had the Roma ever expressed any interest in becoming farmers. To ensure Roma compliance, the Empress put restrictions on their nomadic life and their use of the Romani language. The attempt was a dismal failure.

With the fall of communism, many European governments tried again to integrate the Roma into "mainstream" society. Nomadism was ended in many places by the issuing of state decrees and the Roma were encouraged, and sometimes forced,

Roma fear the loss of a centuries-old way of life, and resist the efforts of countries trying to integrate them into mainstream society.

to adopt non-Roma ways of life. The problem with this approach was that the Roma did not—and do not—want to give up their language, their customs, their ways of life, or their sense of community.

Historian Crowe offers his opinion on why assimilation has repeatedly failed. "It is impossible to expect a group that has spent centuries on the periphery of society suddenly or comfortably to adapt to a completely new educational and social environment, particularly when this minority is saddled with poverty."[84]

Isabel Fonseca agrees: "Reformers through time . . . no doubt believed that such measures would greatly improve the difficult lives of Gypsies. . . . But no one ever thought to ask the Gypsies [what they wanted] and accordingly all efforts at assimilation failed."[85]

Racism and Discrimination

Another difficulty facing the governments who have tried to integrate the Roma into society has been the rampant racism and discrimination that still exists throughout the world. No matter where the Roma live or try to go, they continue to face widespread distrust, hatred, racial discrimination, and violence.

Often tormented by local officials, the police, and townspeople, it is difficult for the Roma to get jobs, earn an honest living, or live comfortably even within their own communities. Public opinion polls taken in many European countries in the twenty-first century still show almost universal hatred of the Roma.

In a 2001 interview on National Public Radio, an elderly Hungarian woman reflected an opinion that is widely shared by the majority of people in Eastern Europe. She stated: "I can say that there are very few out of this Roma community who can be considered as human beings. Most of them are just stealing, robbing, and doing bad things all the time. I can tell you that it's horrible. It's impossible to live together with them."[86]

These opinions are shared by scholars, priests, and government officials throughout Europe and the world. According to *Economist* journalists, Slovakia's former prime minister, Vladimir Meciar, for example, once described the Roma as "mental retards."[87] And in an interview with Isabel Fonseca, an Eastern European priest stated: "Even God is fed up with the Gypsies. They are pagans, heathens."[88]

The Roma have faced these kinds of charges throughout their history. An unidentified Gypsy woman, interviewed by journalist Peter Maas, stated in the 1970s: "I recall how we would come into a town and the people yelled 'Lock the doors, the gypsies are coming! Get the children inside, they're going to steal the children. . . . Kill the gypsies, run them out of town, burn them, put them on fire!' Yes, those are my memories."[89]

Negative stereotypes of the Roma persist even among noted scholars and historians. One Roma scholar named Tchalai writes of an interview he and other Roms gave to a well-known historian specializing in Gypsy studies:

A Gypsyologist came in with his notebook in order to ask us questions. Among us were a renowned lawyer, a physician, a company manager, a director of an insurance firm, and even a general. He took us en-bloc for illiterate people. Good savages whose aggressivity had to be tamed. And when we try to show who we are, we cease to be credible, because the idea is deeply rooted that we are a roving race, untamable, outside the norms, and illiterate.[90]

Violence in Eastern Europe

This hatred and suspicion of the Roma, as it has so often in the past, has erupted into many acts of violence in recent years. The statistics for violent incidents against the Roma are startling and disturbing. Since 1990, in the Czech Republic alone, for example, over twelve hundred hate crimes have been reported. Many hundreds of others go unreported because of the Roma's fear of retaliation.

One of the groups who have relentlessly persecuted and attacked the Roma in the last twenty years are the neo-Nazi gangs of youth called "skinheads." Wear-

A painting shows the kind of negative propaganda the Roma face, with its depiction of a Gypsy woman as she attempts to kidnap a child while the girl's father struggles to save her.

been firebombed and there have been numerous Roma deaths as a result of severe and unprovoked beatings.

One of the most shocking cases of anti-Roma violence in Slovakia occurred on July 21, 1995, in the small town of Ziar nad Hronom. According to journalist James Walsh: "Some 30 skinheads threw Molotov cocktails [a homemade bomb] into a Romany hangout, then ran into Mario Goral, 18. As the youth's mother watched in horror from a window, they laughingly set him afire after dousing him with . . . a kind of homemade napalm. Goral died."[92]

It is not just groups like the neo-Nazi skinheads, however, who persecute and attack the Roma. In 1992 Bulgarian police raided a Rom village and violently attacked its inhabitants. Houses were searched, property was damaged, and money and other property were confiscated. A later probe of the incident concluded that the police had done nothing wrong.

And in 1985 an international news agency released the details about a gang of Yugoslav kidnappers working in Austria. The gang was stealing children from Roma homes and selling them to Americans and

ing the swastika, the symbol of the former Nazi party, and shaving their heads, these gangs have become quite common in Europe. "They beat innocent pregnant women, children and elderly people," writes Crowe, "and ransack apartments in Gypsy settlements."[91] Many homes have

The Media

Throughout the years the media, in the form of newspapers, books, and television programs, often have portrayed the Roma in a negative manner. Many of the stereotypes of the Roma as thieves and beggars are the only view presented to the public. Authorities on the Roma offer the opinion that much of the prejudice that exists today against the Roma is due to these kinds of misrepresentations. The Roma also believe that until the world is given an accurate picture of their communities and way of life, it is likely that the persecution and discrimination will continue.

In addition, many acts of violence against the Roma are not reported by the press. As a result, millions of people around the world are unaware of the problems facing the Roma today. Only in the last twenty or thirty years have people in the United States and elsewhere been made aware of the tremendous violence done against the Roma. Throughout Eastern Europe and elsewhere the media has explained the violence and discrimination by claiming that the Roma themselves provoked it.

The same is true in the United States. Most Americans know very little about the actual Roma. They do, however, know a lot about the "Hollywood" Gypsy—a product of the media and the negative stereotypes that have followed the Roma to this country. With very few exceptions, the American media continue to misrepresent the Roma.

An American film actress portrays a stereotypical version of a Gypsy woman.

others. "The parents of the one hundred kidnapped children," writes Ian Hancock, "have been too frightened to report these crimes."[93]

Most of these violent attacks have occurred with little or no restraint from government authorities. In many cases the blame for the violence falls on the Roma, not the aggressors. A policeman in Romania, when interviewed by Isabel Fonseca about these problems in the 1990s, stated: "Killing Gypsies is charity, not murder."[94] His opinion sadly reflects the attitude of many Europeans.

Roma Refugees

As a result of the escalating violence in Eastern Europe, many Roma are now seeking refuge and safe haven elsewhere. Numerous Roma fled to Germany in the early 1990s because of that nation's policies, which were a little more liberal than elsewhere in Europe. Initially allowed asylum in Germany, the Roma in more recent years have increasingly been turned away. Only about 4 percent of the refugees are now admitted. Many of those who are refused admission are instead treated as criminals and sent away in handcuffs, despite their innocence of any wrongdoing. Germany has since passed legislation making it more difficult for Roma refugees to enter their country.

Many Roma have also sought refuge in Great Britain, Canada, and the United States. But even in these democratic countries they are turned away and treated with disdain and prejudice. In 1997 over two

hundred Roma from the Czech Republic and Slovakia disembarked from ferries and asked for asylum in Great Britain. They ran into a wall of hostility and were refused asylum. Refugees arriving in Canada and the United States also have met with many of the same problems.

Thousands of Roma who have fled from Romania and other Eastern European countries in order to escape poverty and persecution now live in refugee settlements located on the borders of many nations. The conditions in these camps are nothing less than deplorable. The United Nations and other organizations have donated food and clothing to many of the ghetto refugees but the situation for the Roma remains critical.

The Growth of Roma Groups

During the last thirty years of the twentieth century, the Roma, for the first time in their history, have begun to make their voices heard throughout the world. One of the first steps toward worldwide recognition was taken in 1971 when an international Gypsy committee organized the First World Romani Congress. Rom delegates from fourteen countries attended this historic meeting, which took place in London.

Five commissions were set up to deal with Roma concerns: social affairs, education, war crimes, language, and culture. The delegates also voted to change their ethnic name from "Gypsy" to "Roma," from the word Romani, the language spoken by the Gypsies. This was done in an

London police evict a large Roma caravan from its encampment. Many Roma have fled Eastern Europe for safer countries such as England, only to encounter more hostility and suspicion.

attempt to give themselves and their communities a name that did not have the negative connotations of the past. Since the 1971 meeting, several other Romani congresses have been held at various locations around the world.

Many Roma organizations exist today that are monitoring Roma civil rights throughout the world. Some of these groups are lobbying for an end to discrimination, while others are negotiating for financial compensation for the victims and survivors of the Holocaust. These groups

include the Ethnic Foundation of the Roma, Young Generations' Roma Society, the Roma Center for Social Interaction, and the Cultural Foundation for the Emancipation of the Roma.

The European Roma Rights Center (ERRC) is another organization that has played an active role in demanding government action in recent years. An international public interest law group that monitors the human and civil rights situation of the Roma throughout Europe, this organization also provides lawyers and legal defenses in cases of human rights abuses. It was set up in Budapest, Hungary, in 1996 and has been successful in keeping hundreds of Roma out of prison for crimes they did not commit.

Young Rom are also beginning to play a more active role in the fight for Rom recognition. They use computers and the Internet to increase the political reach of the Roma and bring worldwide attention to the problems that still exist. In addition, for the first time, many young activists are running for political office in an attempt to voice and promote Roma concerns to European governments.

Roma Success

These Roma groups and others have been successful in several countries in petitioning European governments to act on their behalf. Roma leaders, for instance, approached the Romanian government in 1994, requesting greater human and civil rights for their communities. The government responded with a series of progressive programs, including stricter law enforcement against those individuals and groups who harass and attack the Rom.

In 1985 the Hungarian government, one of the first to do so, established a National Gypsy Council to represent the Roma's concerns. This council assists the Roma in carrying out laws and measures that involve them. And in 1986 the Cultural Association of Gypsies in Hungary was formed to help preserve Roma culture. In the mid-1990s Hungarian leaders also began to crack down on racist groups, at the same time

Roma activists protest at the 2001 World Conference Against Racism. Activists have been making their voices heard since the 1970s.

working to strengthen the minority rights of several groups, including the Roma.

In 1979 the United Nations recognized the Roma as a distinct ethnic group. It was in this same year that a Rom was admitted to the Economic and Social Council of the United Nations as an adviser. In 1991 the United Nations Commission on Human Rights passed a resolution concerning the Roma. It called for the nations of Europe to end the discrimination and persecution of the Roma.

Political Success and the European Union

Another bright spot in Eastern Europe has been the success of various Roma political parties. In 1990 a Rom, Manush Romanov, won a parliamentary seat in Bulgaria; and in 1996 several Roma won seats in the Romanian Parliament. These individuals are playing a significant and successful role in demanding greater Roma rights.

While Roma politicans have begun to have a positive impact on the policies of Eastern European nations, another factor has played an even larger role. This factor is the European Union, an organization of countries working toward the unification of Europe for the purpose of improving the political, economic, and social situation in that part of the world.

Eagerness to join the European Union has caused several Central and Eastern European nations to reexamine their policies toward the Roma. The Union has made it very clear that it will not allow

The Roma and the Vote

Many nations now permit the Roma to vote in state and national elections. There are, however, some notable exceptions. In 1993, for instance, the Czech Republic passed a controversial law that took away the Roma's right to vote. The law, known as the Romany Clause, classified all Roma as foreigners and took away their right to vote and other rights of citizenship. The rationale for this citizenship law was that all citizens and voters had to speak Slovak, something that few Roma are able to do.

In many other countries, the Roma are denied citizenship and the right to vote because of their nomadism. Due to their constant movement from town to town, the Roma are not registered as voters of a particular district or state. Many European countries also fail to include the Roma as an ethnic group when censuses are taken. Because they have historically been denied the vote, Roma have played little to no role in elections. That is beginning to change in many areas of Europe.

these nations entrance until satisfied that the Roma are being given a fair deal.

In the late twentieth century and early twenty-first century, many issues involving the Roma were addressed by various national and international organizations. These organizations, both Roma and non-Roma, are working to strengthen Roma cultural identity and encourage the Roma to participate in local and national politics.

But, writes Crowe: "Until [all] the . . . government[s of Eastern Europe] decide to adopt policies designed to address the special needs of the Gypsy community, that demonstrate respect for their unique traditions, and [establish] a serious campaign to combat prejudice against them, . . . [the] Roma will find it difficult to play a larger part in [the] new democrac[ies.][95]

In the early years of the new millennium, the Roma still face a multitude of problems. Despite economic, social, political, and cultural approaches by various organizations in recent years, according to historians, "the Romani people remain the least integrated and most persecuted people of Europe."[96]

Chapter 7

The Roma in the Twenty-First Century

Day-to-day life for the Roma, never easy, continues to be difficult in the twenty-first century. In addition to widespread discrimination and persecution, the Roma face a multiplicity of problems that leave them struggling to survive in modern society. According to journalist William J. Kole, "From Budapest to Bucharest, from Plovdiv to Prague, life for Eastern Europe's . . . Gypsies is no easier in the new millennium than it was in the last one."[97]

Poverty and Unemployment

Most of the Roma in Eastern Europe and elsewhere live in poverty and are dependent on welfare to provide even the most basic of their needs. Their health and living standards are usually well below national averages. Journalist James Walsh elaborates: "In central and eastern Europe, real Roma life consists of unemployment, slum housing, discrimination and mob attacks, the likes of which seldom make for news stories farther west."[98]

The statistics are alarming. In Hungary, for instance, according to writer Stephen R. Burant: "About 75% of Gypsies [in 1987] were living at or below the poverty level."[99] Those statistics have not improved in the last fifteen years. In Czechoslovakia there is 70 percent joblessness among the Roma, while the percentage is well over 80 percent in other parts of Eastern Europe. And, according to journalists for the *Economist*, "In Romania's wretched orphanages, three-fourths of the inhabitants are Gypsies."[100]

An unidentified Rom in Eastern Europe told Walsh: "As a Roma, I don't have a chance. If I go to a restaurant, they refuse to serve me. If I look for a job, they refuse to hire me."[101] With minimal skills, education, and training, those few Roma who do have jobs are usually the first to lose them during hard economic times. According to another Rom, interviewed by journalist Kole: "Once they see we're Gypsies, they don't even want to talk to us."[102]

Journalist Peter S. Green agrees. He writes: "Except for a handful of Gypsy intellectuals—doctors, lawyers, and politicians—Gypsies are at the bottom rungs of Romanian society, holding the jobs no one else wants, such as rag pickers, pot menders, and migrant farm workers."[103]

Health Care and Imprisonment

The statistics are just as bad when it comes to Roma health care and imprisonment. Journalist Emil Ginter writes: "Health policymakers and researchers have paid little attention to the health needs of Roma people."[104] According to a 1983 report by the group Save the Children, the infant mortality rate among the Roma in Great Britain is fifteen times higher than the national average. Isabel Fonseca adds that throughout Europe, "their lives are about a third shorter than those of their countrymen."[105]

Also, a disproportionate number of Roma end up in prison. According to Bulgarian statistics nearly 80 percent of all prison inmates in that nation are Gypsies. The Roma are blamed for a variety of criminal acts, from the lesser charges of begging and picking pockets to the more serious charges of murder and kidnapping. They often are innocent of any wrongdoing

These Roma eke out a living in Romania by collecting and selling recyclable materials. Many Roma live in poverty.

The Roma "Nobility"

While the majority of the Roma living in Europe live in poverty, a small minority have managed to amass great wealth. Two such individuals are Florin Cioba and Iulian Radulescu, members of a small upper class in Romania's Roma community.

Florin Cioba is known to many as the "International King of the Gypsies." He is not a real monarch, although he is an extremely influential and prosperous leader in his community. He crowned himself "king" in 1997. A Pentecostal minister, Florin Cioba followed in the footsteps of his fa-

ther Ioan who "became" king in 1992. The elder Cioba is credited with establishing the first adult education centers for the Roma in Romania and fighting to have Roma children accepted into state schools.

Roma "Emperor" Iulian Radulescu holds court at his palace in Sibiu, Romania, a few houses down from his rival, Cioba. He crowned himself "Emperor" in 1993, donning a crown made up of forty gold coins and adorned with rubies and diamonds. The crown has an estimated worth of nearly $90 million.

but end up serving long sentences in prison. In addition, the police and legal systems also tend to punish the Roma far more severely for lesser crimes than mainstream members of society are punished for serious crimes.

Life on the Road

During the last fifty years European governments have made it difficult for the Roma to maintain their nomadic life. In 1958, for example, a Czechoslovakian law banned nomadism. According to Roma sources: "To enforce this policy, police killed all caravan horses and removed the wheels from their wagons. To remain a nomad was punishable by prison terms of six months to three years."[106]

While most Roma would prefer to maintain their traditional nomadic life, only a small minority actually continues to pursue this lifestyle. While the numbers of nomads have dropped in recent years, thousands of Roma still spend their summers in colorful motor homes and trailers traveling throughout Europe. Going from one small village market to another, they sell cloth, clothing, and other goods. In the winter, however, many of the Roma live in dingy apartments or ghettoes in towns and cities.

The same is true in the United States. Spending the winter in the warmer climate of Florida, the Roma travel in the spring to the Midwest states where they work as seasonal fruit and vegetable pickers. They generally head east in the summer, often spending those months in New Jersey picking cranberries and other fruits before retiring south again for the winter.

Today, many of the Roma travel in trucks, often towing large caravans. "When parked," writes G.A.C. Binnie, "they are usually seen in lay-bys or on waste ground with lots of dogs, children and rubbish. In these unofficial caravan sites, they live in squalor and the type of conditions prevailing in this country a couple of centuries ago."[107] Even so, their traveling life is often preferable to the kinds of housing available to the Gypsies.

Housing

The majority of Roma now live in permanent settlements. Housing in these areas is minimal and substandard. In Eastern Europe many live on the outskirts of villages and small towns. Hundreds of residents are crammed into run-down shacks made of logs and mud. Many homes have bare, dirt floors, while few have plumbing or running water. According to *National Geographic* journalist Peter Godwin, who visited many of these homes during his travels with Roma families, "It is a scene of medieval squalor."[108]

Limited employment opportunities and low Rom salaries are to blame in part for the substandard housing. More frequently, however, these kinds of homes are the only ones available to the Roma. In Italy, for instance, where nearly one hundred thousand Roma live, most do not qualify for public housing because of their no-

madic way of life. The Italian government has responded by providing a complex of ghettos for those Roma who have settled down. These ghettos are located in areas of town separate from the majority of homes. Inadequate funding to Roma projects by the Italian government has resulted in deplorable conditions in these remote ghetto areas.

The same is true elsewhere in Europe. The town of Kalistra in southern Hungary, according to National Public Radio, is typical of ghetto life. "Its two thousand Roma have been pushed out into an outlying ghetto. The buildings are ramshackle and small. There's no electricity, no running water, no sanitation."[109]

Even more disturbing is a Roma ghetto in Slovakia. This particular settlement is located on the site of an old arsenic mine. The Roma who live there are constantly exposed to the poisons in the ground and the air.

Roma groups and organizations are speaking out today about the intolerable housing and living conditions available to the Gypsies. One such group, the Democratic Alliance of Hungarian Gypsies, was created in the late 1980s. "Among its goals," writes David M. Crowe, "was the creation of Gypsy settlements throughout Hungary."[110]

One such settlement can be found in the village of Shuto Orizar. Home to around thirty thousand individuals, the village has schools, a medical clinic, a movie house, and a sports stadium, all for the exclusive use of the Roma. Sadly, this kind of settlement is the exception rather than the rule.

Housing conditions in most Roma communities, like this one, are deplorable.

Education

Historically, the Roma have never placed much importance on formal public education. Their children learned everything they needed to know in their homes and communities. Today, however, Roma children are required to go to school by the various countries in which they live. Unfortunately, the children usually meet resistance, prejudice, and difficulty wherever they go.

According to historians: "Before World War II, nearly all Roma were illiterate and, faced with the discrimination they felt in gadje society, had no motiv-ation to educate themselves, as even with an education, they would have difficulty finding a place in society."[111] Little has changed.

It is estimated, according to the Save the Children organization, that "across East [Europe], one-half of all Gypsy children never attend school or are forced into institutions for the mentally deficient."[112] Many of the remainder drop out of school after a few years of education. Many of these dropouts do so because of persecution and bullying from non-Roma students.

Roma children are often viewed as "problem" children by public officials and automatically placed in remedial classes. One reason for this placement is that large numbers of Roma children are unable to speak their country's language.

Another problem is that many Rom schools, according to journalists and eye-witnesses, are more like orphanages and juvenile detention centers than they are schools. These various problems have resulted in staggering illiteracy rates of 50 percent and upward.

An additional problem has developed within the last twenty years. "In the very few cases where individuals are properly educated," writes Isabel Fonseca, "they usually tend to leave the Gypsy community."[113] Their departure means that there is little hope of them passing on their knowledge to future generations of Roma children.

Educational Advancements

Special interest groups who are now fighting for the Roma all agree that education is the key to improving their status. Among other things, these groups are now demanding literacy classes for adults. They

Education for the Roma in the United States

Education for the Roma who live in the United States lags far behind that of other ethnic groups. It has been estimated, in fact, that nearly 95 percent of the Roma who live in America are illiterate, a number far exceeding that of any other group.

Many American state governments have made positive attempts to alleviate this situation. The state of Texas has had more success than most and it has one of the largest Roma populations in the United States. While Houston and Fort Worth have the largest numbers, nearly every large town in Texas has some Roma residents.

The government of Texas made many early attempts to establish primary and el-ementary schools for the Romani. For example, in the 1970s a mobile Romani language school traveled between the big cities in that state. This innovative idea helped bring literacy in both English and Romani to large segments of Texas's Roma community. Changes in governmental policies, however, eventually curtailed these plans and programs.

In addition, the University of Texas has one of the largest collections of Romani cultural materials in the world. Today, that university is the only institution of higher learning in the United States that offers courses in Romani language, culture, and history. This groundbreaking program has attracted scholars from around the world.

also want Rom history taught in those countries with large Roma populations.

There are now preschool programs available for Roma children in several European countries, most notably the Czech Republic, Hungary, and Slovakia. Prior to starting elementary school, Romani-speaking youngsters are helped in these preschools to learn the main language of the country in which they live.

Progress also has been made in other areas. More Roma teaching assistants have been hired in some countries, while else-where a few governments provide money for school lunches. In addition, many schools are now offering a more progressive curriculum that includes Roma history. Many Roma today are relearning the Romani language after many years of having been forbidden to speak it.

Many elementary schoolbooks in parts of Europe are now being written in both the local language and Romani. New scholarships are available for Roma students interested in continuing their education. And in the late 1990s the Roman-

Two Roma classmates work at the blackboard in a special Hungarian school in 1998.

ian government established "Caravan Classrooms." These special classrooms are mobile and follow the Roma on their journeys while providing education to Rom children.

Before real success in education is possible, however, historians say: "The gadje will have to overcome their long hostility toward and misunderstanding of the Roma; and Roma parents will have to overcome their fear of corruption [and violence] by the non-Roma."[114]

Roma Participation in Mainstream Society

The Roma continue to practice a wide variety of different crafts and occupations. Many have continued their interest in horses and a few own their own horse-breeding farms, taking their animals to horse fairs all across the globe. Others tour in song and dance groups. Still others have gone on to professional careers. Many Roma women continue to tell fortunes, usually working at carnivals and circuses.

The Roma, however, have had to abandon many of their old trades. According to an unidentified Roma,

Traditional Gypsy skills such as . . . [metalworking] have become redundant in an industrial age. In many countries, Romany people are becoming assimilated into society as unskilled labor. Our survival, therefore, depends as it has always on finding an economic niche for ourselves so that we can maintain our economic and cultural independence from mainstream society.[115]

Pepe La Fleur, a European Gypsy, stated in an interview with *National Geographic* journalist Peter Godwin:

The old ways are over. We didn't used to go to school. We traveled constantly and we were always chased away from one town to the next, and often we had to hide in the forest. It's better now . . . but in a few years there will be no Gypsies left here [in France.] They are all buying houses and living differently. They are mixing with other kids and intermarrying, and the culture is becoming diluted.[116]

Other Roma have a less pessimistic point of view. "Many Roma," write Roma authorities, "are [for the first time] integrating and participating in the mainstream of European and American culture without compromising their identity."[117]

Roma Arts and Culture

While adapting to European and American ways of life, the Roma have maintained many of their rich cultural and artistic traditions. Gypsy musicians, for instance, continue to entertain in cafes, taverns, and restaurants around the world. Roma authors, poets, and journalists are being read by increasingly large numbers of people, both Roma and non-Roma. In addition, Roma theater groups, especially in Russia, are winning worldwide acclaim.

The Roma in America

It is estimated that over one million Roma reside in the United States. This number comprises several groups, each having its own cultural, linguistic, and historical tradition. One is the Ludar, a group of Roma who emigrated from Bosnia. Most Ludar Roma earn their livings as animal trainers and showpeople, working in traveling circuses and carnivals around the United States.

Another group is the Romnichels, Roma who emigrated from England. Other populations include the Kalderasha, Machwaya, and the Bashalde. There is little contact among these different groups of Roma, owing primarily to the significant differences in their language dialects.

Even today the Roma, as an ethnic group, are not found on any census or immigration statistics. They are in many ways an invisible people, preferring to keep to themselves and live in their own communities.

American Rom George Kaslov, whose grandfather arrived in the United States a century ago from Russia, was interviewed by *National Geographic* journalist Peter Godwin for an article entitled "Gypsies" which appeared in 2001. Kaslov stated: "There's a will within us to survive as a people. All the other ethnic groups who came to America, they tend to assimilate after a few generations. They lose their customs and language. But not the Rom."

An American Roma child of the 1940s stands by a sign advertising palm reading.

The Roma theater tradition dates back to the 1930s when Soviet officials supported the creation of a theater dedicated to the creation of plays about the Roma way of life. The official opening of the Moscow Gypsy Theatre Romen (or Theatre Romen), the first of its kind anywhere in the world, was held on January 24, 1931.

Audiences in Moscow were captivated by Gypsy music and the authentic Roma costumes. The theater became an almost instantaneous success with its performances of *Life on Wheels* and *Today and Tomorrow.* "For the first time in their history," writes actor Nikolai Slichenko, "the Gypsies could describe on stage in their mother tongue what was most important in their lives."[118]

The Theatre Romen continued to perform during World War II, touring more than sixty places in Siberia and other areas of the Soviet Union. Upon their return to Moscow, the theater cast was awarded the "Defense of the Caucasus" medal for their bravery during the war.

The Theatre has gone on to become one of the most prominent institutions in Roma cultural history. Their most important tour in recent years was the one they made to Japan in 1982. This represented their first performance outside the Soviet Union. With over fifteen plays in their repertoire, the members of the Theatre Romen continue to entertain audiences today. According to Yugoslavian Roma artist Dragan Ristic, "This institution will continue to play a significant role in the cultural life of the Roma [for generations to come.]"[119]

The Roma Today

While facing a myriad of economic, social, and discriminatory problems, the Roma, nonetheless, look optimistically—but realistically—to the future. "The Roma are a people," write historians, "who in spite of suffering a millennium of racism . . . and now poverty, maintain sound family values, [and] remain loyal to both community and country."[120]

Many Roma are somewhat less optimistic about the problems still facing them. For instance, the Roma have long demanded official minority status in order to obtain government support and funding. The funding, in particular, is needed to preserve Roma cultural, linguistic, and historic traditions. But, according to historian David M. Crowe: "Official unwillingness to grant this status underscores a lack of commitment to anything other than to transform the Roma into little Hungarians, Romanians, or Russians."[121]

Roma activist and politician Manush Romanov of Bulgaria voiced the opinion of many Roma when he spoke at an international meeting of the Roma in 1992. He stated: "We want separate schools, our own languages taught in these schools, and our own villages. We must build houses for our people. We must have our own homes for our own way of life."[122]

Most Roma politicians and activists agree that there can be no acceptance for their people until the officials and citizens

A Roma family on the move. After enduring centuries of persecution, their indomitable culture is on the long road to a brighter future.

of the world address the deep and powerful prejudice that still exists against the Roma. The issues of poverty and unemployment must also be considered. Above all, the Roma want non-Roma governments and communities to acknowledge the many centuries of racism, slavery, prejudice, and persecution.

Hope for the Future

The Roma face a long and difficult road ahead, but there is hope on the horizon. As Isabel Fonseca writes: "The Gypsies [have] experienced centuries of chaos, of social fragmentation, and instability. . . . Now they [are] making their case, and making it publicly."[123] And more importantly, the world is beginning to listen.

Historian David M. Crowe agrees: "A new Roma awakening has emerged that has seen a flurry of political, social, and cultural organizations develop that offer the Gypsies new choices for the first time in [their] history."[124]

The Roma have survived over five hundred years of suffering, while continuing to adapt to changing conditions and diffi-cult times. "There are some fifteen million Roms dispersed across the world," stated former prime minister of India, Indira Gandhi, in 1983: "Their history is one of suffering and misery, but it is also one of the victories of the human spirit over the blows of fate. Today the Rom revive their culture and are looking for their identity. If they are understood by their fellow citizens in their new homelands, their culture will enrich the society's atmosphere."[125]

Notes

Introduction

1. James Riordan, *Russian Gypsy Tales.* Brooklyn, NY: Interlink Books, 1992, p. ix.
2. *Handbook of Texas Online*, "Roma." www.tsha.utexas.edu.
3. David M. Crowe, *A History of the Gypsies of Eastern Europe and Russia.* New York: St. Martin's Press, 1994, p. 235.
4. Peter Godwin, "Gypsies," *National Geographic*, April 2001, p. 78.
5. Harold Tanner, "The Roma: Persecution," *Patrin Web Journal.* www.patrin.com.
6. *European Roma Rights Center.* www.errc.org.

Chapter 1: The *Romaniya*

7. Eric Solsten and David E. McClure, *Austria: A Country Study.* Washington, DC: Federal Research Division, Library of Congress, 1994, p. 90.
8. W.R. Rishi, "Excerpts from *Roma*," *Romani.org Home Page.* www. romani.org.
9. Ian Hancock, *The Pariah Syndrome: An Account of Gypsy Slavery and Persecution.* Ann Arbor: Karoma, 1989. Reproduced on *Patrin Web Journal*, www.patrin.com.

10. Riordan, *Russian Gypsy Tales*, p. xiv.
11. *Patrin Web Journal*, "Romani Customs and Traditions." www.patrin. com.
12. Isabel Fonseca, *Bury Me Standing: The Gypsies and Their Journey.* New York: Alfred A. Knopf, 1996, p. 80.
13. *Patrin Web Journal*, "Romani Customs and Traditions."
14. *Patrin Web Journal*, "Romani Customs and Traditions."
15. Solsten and McClure, *Austria*, p. 90.
16. Guenter Lewy, *The Nazi Persecution of the Gypsies.* New York: Oxford University Press, 2000, p. 11.
17. Solsten and McClure, *Austria*, p. 90.
18. Lewy, *The Nazi Persecution of the Gypsies*, p. 12.
19. Fonseca, *Bury Me Standing*, p. 54.
20. Solsten and McClure, *Austria*, p. 90.

Chapter 2: Roma Family and Community

21. Fonseca, *Bury Me Standing*, p. 288.
22. Fonseca, *Bury Me Standing*, p. 25.
23. *Patrin Web Journal*, "Romani Customs and Traditions."
24. *Patrin Web Journal*, "Romani Customs and Traditions."

25. *Patrin Web Journal*, "Romani Customs and Traditions."
26. *Patrin Web Journal*, "Romani Customs and Traditions."
27. Fonseca, *Bury Me Standing*, p. 44.
28. *Patrin Web Journal*, "Romani Customs and Traditions."
29. Fonseca, *Bury Me Standing*, p. 44.
30. Peter Maas, *King of the Gypsies*. New York: Viking Press, 1974, p. 8.
31. Solsten and McClure, *Austria*, p. 90.

Chapter 3: Spirituality and the Arts
32. *Patrin Web Journal*, "Romani Customs and Traditions."
33. Fonseca, *Bury Me Standing*, p. 48.
34. Fonseca, *Bury Me Standing*, p. 248.
35. Fonseca, *Bury Me Standing*, p. 247.
36. Fonseca, *Bury Me Standing*, p. 248.
37. *Patrin Web Journal*, "Romani Customs and Traditions."
38. *Patrin Web Journal*, "Romani Customs and Traditions."
39. *Patrin Web Journal*, "Romani Customs and Traditions."
40. Dork Zygotian, "A Vanishing Tradition," *Patrin Web Journal*, www.patrin.com.
41. *The World Book Encyclopedia of People and Places: D to H*. Chicago: World Books, 2000, p. 599.
42. *Romani.org Home Page* "Romani Dance Page." www.romani.org.

Chapter 4: The Early Years
43. *Romani.org Home Page* "Opre Roma!" www.romani.org.

44. Bart McDowell, *Gypsies: Wanderers of the World*. Washington, DC: National Geographic Books, 1970, p. 22.
45. *Radio Prague*, "The History of the Roma Minority in the Czech Republic." *www.romove.cz.*
46. Crowe, *A History of the Gypsies of Eastern Europe and Russia*, p. 37.
47. Maas, *King of the Gypsies*, p. 50.
48. Ian Hancock, "The Roma: Myth and Reality," *Patrin Web Journal*, www.patrin.com.
49. Riordan, *Russian Gypsy Tales*, p. xiv.
50. Crowe, *A History of the Gypsies of Eastern Europe and Russia*, p. 235.
51. Hancock, *The Pariah Syndrome*, chap. 15.
52. Fonseca, *Bury Me Standing*, p. 229.
53. *Radio Prague*, "The History of the Roma Minority in the Czech Republic."
54. *Radio Prague*, "The History of the Roma Minority in the Czech Republic."
55. Fonseca, *Bury Me Standing*, p. 178.
56. Hancock, *The Pariah Syndrome*.
57. Hancock, *The Pariah Syndrome*.
58. Hancock, *The Pariah Syndrome*.

Chapter 5: *O Porraimos*, The Holocaust and Its Aftermath
59. Lewy, *The Nazi Persecution of the Gypsies*, p. 3.
60. *Association of Gypsies/Romani International*, "Hidden Victims: The Unknown Assault on Europe's Gyp-

sies." http://198.62.75.1/www2/gypsies.net.

61. Lewy, *The Nazi Persecution of the Gypsies*, p. 4.

62. Lewy, *The Nazi Persecution of the Gypsies*, p. 1.

63. Tanner, "The Roma: Persecution," *Patrin Web Journal*.

64. *Economist*, "A Gypsy Awakening." September 11, 1999.

65. Fonseca, *Bury Me Standing*, p. 268.

66. Fonseca, *Bury Me Standing*, p. 243.

67. Deborah Dwork and Robert Jan van Pelt, *Auschwitz*. New York: W.W. Norton and Company, 1996, p. 320.

68. Lewy, *The Nazi Persecution of the Gypsies*, p. 14.

69. Ian Hancock, "Genocide of the Roma in the Holocaust," *Patrin Web Journal*, www.patrin.com.

70. Lewy, *The Nazi Persecution of the Gypsies*, p. 162.

71. McDowell, *Gypsies*, p. 66.

72. McDowell, *Gypsies*, p. 65.

73. *Association of Gypsies/Romani International*, "Hidden Victims."

74. *Radio Prague*, "The History of the Roma Minority in the Czech Republic."

75. Fonseca, *Bury Me Standing*, p. 274.

76. *Association of Gypsies/Romani International*, "Hidden Victims."

77. Hancock, "Genocide of the Roma in the Holocaust."

78. Tanner, "The Roma Persecution."

79. Crowe, *A History of the Gypsies of Eastern Europe and Russia*, p. 22.

Chapter 6: A Hostile World

80. Noah Adams and Linda Wertheimer, "Profile: Treatment of the Roma in Europe," *All Things Considered*, National Public Radio, September 5, 2001.

81. Fonseca, *Bury Me Standing*, p. 140.

82. Crowe, *A History of the Gypsies of Eastern Europe and Russia*, p. xv.

83. Crowe, *A History of the Gypsies of Eastern Europe and Russia*, p. 44.

84. Crowe, *A History of the Gypsies of Eastern Europe and Russia*, p. 64.

85. Fonseca, *Bury Me Standing*, p. 8.

86. Adams and Wertheimer, "Profile."

87. *Economist*, "A Gypsy Awakening."

88. Fonseca, *Bury Me Standing*, p. 168.

89. Maas, *King of the Gypsies*, p. 87.

90. Tchalai, "Preface to the Tzigane Tarot," *Romani.org Home Page*, July 1984. www.romani.org.

91. Crowe, *A History of the Gypsies of Eastern Europe and Russia*, p. 104.

92. James Walsh, "Europe: Outcasts of Europe." *Time International*, November 3, 1997.

93. Hancock, *The Pariah Syndrome*.

94. Isabel Fonseca, "Europe: Viewpoint: At the Bottom of the Heap" *Time International*, November 3, 1997.

95. Crowe, *A History of the Gypsies of Eastern Europe and Russia*, p. 30.

96. *Patrin Web Journal*, "A Brief History of the Roma." www.patrin.com.

Chapter 7: The Roma in the Twenty-First Century

97. William J. Kole, "Across Eastern Europe, Gypsies' Fortunes Have Never Been Bleaker." *AP Worldstream*, April 8, 2002.

98. Walsh, "Europe."

99. Stephen R. Burant, *Hungary: A Country Study*. Washington, DC: Federal Research Division, Library of Congress, 1990, p. 78.

100. *Economist*, "A Gypsy Awakening."

101. Walsh, "Europe."

102. Kole, "Across Eastern Europe, Gypsies' Fortunes Have Never Been Bleaker."

103. Peter S. Green. "The Nomads of Eastern Europe." *U.S. News and World Report*, October 26, 1992.

104. G.A.C. Binnie and Emil Ginter, "The Health of Gypsies," *British Medical Journal*. http://bmj.com.

105. Fonseca, *Bury Me Standing*, p. 15.

106. *Patrin Web Journal*, "Timeline of Romani History." www.patrin.com.

107. Binnie and Ginter, "The Health of Gypsies."

108. Godwin, "Gypsies," p. 85.

109. Adams and Wertheimer, "Profile."

110. Crowe, *A History of the Gypsies of Eastern Europe and Russia*, p. 102.

111. *Radio Prague*, "The History of the Roma Minority in the Czech Republic."

112. Kole, "Across Eastern Europe, Gypsies' Fortunes Have Never Been Bleaker."

113. Fonseca, *Bury Me Standing*, p. 9.

114. *Patrin Web Journal*, "Romani Customs and Traditions."

115. Jake Bowers-Burbridge, "Back to the Road," *Rom News*, www.romnews.com.

116. Godwin, "Gypsies," p. 82.

117. *Patrin Web Journal*, "Romani Customs and Traditions."

118. Nikolai Slichenko, "From Campfire to Footlights: Gypsies in the Theater," *Patrin Web Journal*, www.patrin.com.

119. Dragan Ristic, "The History of Theatre Romen," *Patrin Web Journal*, www.patrin.com.

120. *Romani World*. www.romaniworld.com.

121. Crowe, *A History of the Gypsies of Eastern Europe and Russia*, p. 238.

122. Fonseca, *Bury Me Standing*, p. 299.

123. Fonseca, *Bury Me Standing*, p. 300.

124. Crowe, *A History of the Gypsies of Eastern Europe and Russia*, p. xvi.

125. *Romani.org Home Page*, "Opre Roma!"

For Further Reading

Geography Department, *Romania.* Minneapolis, MN: Lerner, 1993. This book offers a look at the history and people of Romania, including a good deal of information about the Gypsies.

Harold Greenfeld, *Gypsies.* New York: Crown, 1977. This is an excellent book that focuses on all aspects of Gypsy history and culture.

Judy L. Hasday, *The Holocaust.* Philadelphia: Chelsea House, 2002. An excellent book that offers an overview of the Nazi persecution of Jews, Gypsies, and other ethnic groups during World War II.

Michael Leapman, *Witnesses to War.* London: Viking, 1998. The author presents eight true-life stories of those persecuted by the Nazis during World War II, including one Gypsy account.

Richard Steins, *Hungary: Crossroads of Europe.* New York: Marshall Cavenish, 1997. The author presents an overall look at the country of Hungary, its history, and its people.

Terri Willis, *Romania.* New York: Childrens Press, 2001. This book presents a look at Romania with numerous references to the Gypsies who make up Romania's largest minority group.

Works Consulted

Books

Stephen R. Burant, *Hungary: A Country Study*. Washington, DC: Federal Research Division, Library of Congress, 1990. The book offers a comprehensive look at the history, government, and people of Hungary.

David M. Crowe, *A History of the Gypsies of Eastern Europe and Russia*. New York: St. Martin's Press, 1994. This excellent book looks at the cultural and historical traditions of the Gypsies in Eastern Europe and Russia. The author takes an especially close look at the revival of prejudice and the plight of the Roma today.

Glenn E. Curtis, *Bulgaria: A Country Study*. Washington, DC: Federal Research Division, Library of Congress, 1993. The author focuses on the history, government, and people of Bulgaria.

———, *Russia: A Country Study*. Washington, DC: Federal Research Division, Library of Congress, 1998. A comprehensive study of Russia, its history, government, and people.

———, *Yugoslavia: A Country Study*. Washington, DC: Federal Research Division, Library of Congress, 1992. The author offers a comprehensive look at Yugoslavia, its history, government, and people.

Deborah Dwork and Robert Jan van Pelt, *Auschwitz*. New York: W.W. Norton and Company, 1996. The authors present a comprehensive look at the history of this notorious concentration camp, including the extermination of both Jews and Gypsies.

Isabel Fonseca, *Bury Me Standing: The Gypsies and Their Journey*. New York: Alfred A. Knopf, 1996. The author, in this excellent and insightful book, lived and traveled with many different groups of Gypsies throughout Eastern Europe.

Guenter Lewy, *The Nazi Persecution of the Gypsies*. New York: Oxford University Press, 2000. The author, using thousands of documents from German and Austrian archives, creates an accurate and disturbing picture of the persecution of the Gypsies throughout history and most notably during World War II.

Peter Maas, *King of the Gypsies.* New York: Viking, 1974. Maas, the author of *Serpico*, in this controversial book presents an often derogatory look at Gypsy life in the United States, including the infighting that has occurred for leadership among one particular group of Roma.

Bart McDowell, *Gypsies: Wanderers of the World.* Washington, DC: National Geographic Books, 1970. The author embarks on a journey with a group of Gypsies through Europe and the world, including a trip to India to seek their roots.

James Riordan, *Russian Gypsy Tales.* Brooklyn, NY: Interlink Books, 1992. The author presents numerous Gypsy folktales told throughout the ages by the Roma of Russia.

Eric Solsten and David E. McClure, *Austria: A Country Study.* Washington, DC: Federal Research Division, Library of Congress, 1994. This book offers a comprehensive look at Austria, its history, government, and people.

Nicole Williams, *Romania and Moldova.* Oakland, CA: Lonely Planet, 1998. The author, who lives in Romania, writes of the history and people of these two countries, including several excellent references to the Gypsies.

The World Book Encyclopedia of People and Places: D to H. Chicago: World Book, 2000. This reference volume contains an excellent section on the Gypsies of Eastern Europe.

Periodicals

Noah Adams and Linda Wertheimer. "Profile: Treatment of the Roma in Europe," *All Things Considered*, National Public Radio, September 5, 2001.

Sarah Chayes and Jacki Lyden, "Gypsies," *Weekend All Things Considered*, National Public Radio, August 29, 1998.

Economist, "Europe: Go to School and Stay There; Gypsy Children," December 1, 2001.

Economist, "A Gypsy Awakening," September 11, 1999.

Economist, "Persecuted Britons." May 30, 1998.

Economist, "Slovakia's Unloved Ones." March 4, 2000.

Isabel Fonseca, "Europe: Viewpoint: At the Bottom of the Heap," *Time International*, November 3, 1997.

Peter Godwin, "Gypsies," *National Geographic*, April 2001.

Peter S. Green, "The Nomads of Eastern Europe," *U.S. News and World Report*, October 26, 1992.

William J. Kole, "Across Eastern Europe, Gypsies' Fortunes Have Never Been Bleaker," *AP Worldstream*, April 8, 2002.

James Walsh, "Europe: Outcasts of Europe." *Time International*, November 3, 1997.

Women's Review of Books, "They Couldn't Take Our Thoughts," March 1, 1995.

Internet Sources
Association of Gypsies/Romani International, "Hidden Victims: The Unknown Assault on Europe's Gypsies." http://198.62.75.1/ www2/gypsies.net.

G.A.C. Binnie and Emil Ginter, "The Health of Gypsies," *British Medical Journal*. http://bmj.com.

Jake Bowers-Burbridge, "Back to the Road," *Rom News*. www.romnews.com.

Michael Dregni, "Django," *Gypsy Jazz Website*. www.hotclub. co.uk.

Gypsy Lore Society, "Information on Gypsy and Traveler Cultures." www.gypsyloresociety.org.

Ian Hancock, "Genocide of the Roma in the Holocaust," *Patrin Web Journal*. www.patrin.com.

———, *The Pariah Syndrome: An Account of Gypsy Slavery and Persecution*. Ann Arbor: Karoma, 1989. Reproduced on *Patrin Web Journal,* www.patrin.com.

———, "The Roma: Myth and Reality," *Patrin Web Journal*. www.patrin.com.

Handbook of Texas Online, "Roma." www.tsha.utexas.edu.

Patrin Web Journal, "A Brief History of the Roma." www.patrin.com.

Patrin Web Journal, "Romani Customs and Traditions." www.patrin.com.

Patrin Web Journal, "Timeline of Romani History." www.patrin.com.

Radio Prague, "The History of the Roma Minority in the Czech Republic." www.romove.cz.

W.R. Rishi, "Excerpts from Roma," *Romani.org Home Page*. www.romani.org.

Dragan Ristic, "The History of the Theatre Romen," *Patrin Web Journal*. www.patrin.com.

Romani.org Home Page, "Opre Roma!" www.romani.org.

Romani.org Home Page, "Romani Dance Page." www.romani.org.

Nikolai Slichenko, "From Campfire to Footlights: Gypsies in the Theater," *Patrin Web Journal*. www.patrin.com.

Harold Tanner, "The Roma: Persecution," *Patrin Web Journal*. www.patrin.com.

Tchalai, "Preface to the Tzigane Tarot," *Romani.org Home Page*, July 1984. www.romani.org.

Dork Zygotian, "A Vanishing Tradition," *Patrin Web Journal*. www.patrin.com.

Websites

European Roma Rights Center (www.errc.org). This center is an international law organization whose members monitor Roma human and civil rights.

Romani World (www.romaniworld.com). This home page provides access to other sites that concentrate on the Roma in Europe.

Index

Picture Credits

Cover Photo: © David and Peter Turnley/CORBIS
© Associated Press, AP, 83, 86, 88, 92
© Bettmann/CORBIS, 29, 39, 42, 45
© Dean Conger/CORBIS, 22
© CORBIS, 90
Jeff Di Matteo, 50
© Jerzy Ficowski/USHMM Photo Archives, 66
© Fine Art Photographic Library/Art Resource, NY, 11
© Hulton Archive, 14, 17, 33, 34, 43, 46, 61, 69, 73, 78
© John Springer Collection/CORBIS, 76
© Lawrence Manning/CORBIS, 30
© Mary Evans Picture Library, 53, 54, 56, 75
© Reunion des Musees Nationaux/Art Resource, NY, 23
© Reuters NewMedia Inc./CORBIS, 79
© Scala/Art Resource, NY, 51
© Peter Turnley/CORBIS, 19, 27
© Yad Vashem Photo Archives/USHMM Photo Archives, 63

About the Author

Anne Wallace Sharp is the author of one adult book, *Gifts*, a compilation of stories about hospice patients, and several children's books, including *Daring Women Pirates* and four other books for Lucent Books. In addition, she has written numerous magazine articles for both the adult and children's market. A retired registered nurse, Sharp has a degree in history and a strong interest in indigenous people. Her other interests include reading, traveling, and spending time with her two grandchildren, Jacob and Nicole. Sharp lives in Beavercreek, Ohio.